76 recipes for kids ages 2-8

our thanks to
zenobia cambric
ruth ingram
anna joseph
and to the parents and children
at grove parent nursery school
who gamely tried everything,
the bad ideas as well as the good,
and gave us this remembrance
of those good years

barbara wilms
barbara stross
robin gorton

Crunchy bananas

and other great recipes
kids
can
cook

by barbara wilms

photographs by barbara stross

consultant, robin gorton

sagamore books

salt lake city and santa barbara

1975

sagamore books
a division of peregrine smith, inc.

Wilms, Barbara, 1941-
 Crunchy bananas and other great recipes
 kids can cook.

 1. Cookery—Study and teaching.
I. Stross, Barbara, 1942- ill.   II. Title.
TX661.W62   641.5'02'4054   74-31139
ISBN 0-87905-507-3

contents

introduction

One day, our three-year-old twin boys came home from Grove Parent Nursery School in Berkeley, babbling excitedly over the oysters they had pounded open and fried for a snack that day. They were obviously into something very pleasurable for them, but we were amazed. We had always thought of cooking with children in terms of orange-cashew jello molds made by earnest Girl Scouts in search of merit badges. What could pre-schoolers possibly cook?

A lot, it turned out.

For the rest of the year, teachers Robin Gorton and Dorothy Skaggs did a wide range of cooking projects with three and four-year-olds with occasional help from mothers and fathers. By June, we parents were convinced that cooking is a very nice way to spend time with small boys and girls at home, camping, at a picnic, playground, or school.

Our cookbook came about because we needed recipes and quickly found that not everything works. A sweet potato cookie recipe that sounded promising yet tasted incredibly awful when prepared by pre-schoolers leaps to mind. We found some operations like mashing are beyond most young children. They quickly lose interest in creaming stubborn blobs. On the other hand, they are surprisingly competent with graters and knives.

Over two years, we tested many recipes on offspring, friends, schoolmates, and stray tricycle riders who happened by at the right moment. Feedback from cooks/eaters was immediate, to the point, and totally candid. We put many recipes back in Grandma's file for Grandma to make and chose those in this book for three main reasons—they are easily prepared by children two through eight, they generally appeal to children's tastebuds, and they have some nutritional value.

which recipe

How easy it is for a certain child to prepare a certain recipe depends on his age, how much he has cooked before, and his natural co-ordination; so we've tried to include recipes to fit a wide range of abilities. When choosing a recipe for a child or group, common sense is a pretty good guide. It's also helpful to know that dipping, scrubbing, tearing, pouring, mixing, and spreading are easier than juicing, peeling, cutting, grating, and beating with an egg beater.

Children's taste in foods is hard to predict (barring sweets), but our recipes won approval from nearly everyone who tried them. We noticed that sometimes a negative opinion about a certain food was more a declaration of independence from mother's fond hopes than an honest reaction to how the food tasted. We found if we listened politely to long descriptions about how awful the food was and withheld urgings "to try a bite," most children ate. But a smug I-told-you-so afterwards sabotages this device for all future projects.

Although, generally speaking, the smaller a child, the more open he is to food, a big inducement for any age child is natural pride in his creation. Another impetus to eat comes from what we call the "peer group phenomenon on funny foods." In every group, there was some child who had tried an artichoke, a bean sprout, or a raw pea and could testify to, at the very least, their non-poisonous qualities. We saw these unsophisticated testimonials win over some of the fussiest eaters.

Since children were so inclined to eat, we decided to look for the most nutritious recipes we could find. Most parents whose children were just beginning to discover junk food applauded our efforts and ended up adding another dimension to the children's cooking experience.

travel is broadening

Berkeley, as a university town, has people from many different cultures. Our nursery school class had an American Indian, an eastern Indian, a Chicano, blacks, whites, Japanese/American, Polish, German, and French children. As parents became interested in what we were doing, they brought in family recipes and children cooked them on national holidays such as Cinco de Mayo. We had cornpone and tofu, tortillas and spaetzle, Apache fry bread and greens, and the children learned something about how different people lived. We often looked up countries on maps which the children generally found rather silly ("How can the whole world be on a piece of paper.") but it got them wondering and curiosity is the start of many discoveries.

vocabulary

We learned other interesting facts about cooking with children while searching for good recipes. For example, cooking opens up excellent and completely natural learning situations to children when they're having a good time. We have included a variety of verbs in each recipe so children can have an on-the-job vocabulary lesson as they work. After making vegetable soup, our volunteers could tell us what dice, peel, grate, slice, and measure meant. After peanut butter, they knew grind and stir. Simple victories, but for the young child most concepts are fuzzy before first-hand experience.

math

A child who cooks counts the eggs and teaspoons that go into his mixtures. Two becomes more than the sound he chants between one and three. It has a value. He learns he gets two pieces every time he cuts a lemon or an orange in half. He's meeting fractions casually in a non-threatening way, so when he learns about them formally in grade school he feels comfortable about the concept.

By varying the measurements in a recipe, we tried to give children a number of different counting experiences. For instance, sometimes instead of saying, "Add 1 tablespoon," we called for its equivalent, 3 teaspoons; instead of ⅛ cup, we sometimes asked for 2 tablespoons.

For another kind of counting experience, ask every child to bring in a vegetable for a Community Soup, then make a chart showing the number of people who brought in different ingredients. (Have extra vegetables on hand for kids who forget or those whose families cannot afford to contribute.) Or plot the number of children who cut, sliced, stirred etc.

science

The cooking corner could almost be called a laboratory because opportunities for on-the-spot scientific demonstrations and explanations abound when children cook. Even the youngest is ready to consider some basic ideas like changes from liquid to solid after cooking or refrigeration. Point out those facts with pancakes, bread dough, eggs, and popsicles. Then melt butter on a hot griddle to show how heat can also make a solid liquid.

Older children's curiosity might demand more sophisticated explanations than our book offers, but any library has easy-to-understand science books that are great for the non-scientific parent. Once children have seen the air bubbles in Watch-the-Bubble Pancakes first hand, they can tackle complex explanations with confidence.

It's easy to build on cooking's science lessons or to choose a recipe to illustrate a concept. One simple concrete lesson involves putting an ice cube into a hot frying pan and letting children watch matter change from a solid, to a liquid, to a gaseous state.

Younger children are impressed and get a notion of relative temperatures just from holding ice chips in their hands and seeing them melt. My Own Ice Cream can build nicely on the idea of heat transfer.

Planting seeds is an excellent way for children to get a sense of the cycle of life. Pumpkin seeds make beautiful vines. So do hunks of sweet potatoes suspended in water. Orange, apple, and avocado seeds send up tiny trees. The tops of pineapples develop green leaves in the middle.

A trip to a neighboring garden can also bring the growing information home to a child in a way words cannot.

The day before making Tropical Salad, do an experiment with sugar. Put some cut fruit like strawberries into two different cups. Add nothing to one and a little sugar to the other. After an hour, have children determine which cup holds the most juice. Explain that sugar helps draw the juice out of fruit cells and have an explanation of osmosis ready. (Osmosis takes place when a strong juice such as fruit juice combined with sugar is next to a weak juice such as the strawberry juice still in the fruit. The stronger juice draws the weaker juice out of its cell. That's why we often put sugar on fruit salads if we like them juicy.)

Popcorn is not only a childhood favorite but a dramatic lesson in how heat can make a hard seed kernel explode and let the inside come out. Heat makes the liquid inside a popcorn kernel turn into a gas which takes more room. The pressure grows inside the little kernel until the hard outside shell explodes and all the starch on the inside comes to the outside.

Even gelatin poses a scientific question—why a liquid turned to a solid. Try saying that molecules of gelatin arrange themselves around water so it can't escape. Then the gelatin doesn't seem wet anymore. If the child is in a scientific frame of mind that particular day, you will be into a discussion of microscopes and cells and things too tiny to see with plain eyes.

A science lesson needn't be complicated, because young children are still trying to figure out how the simplest things work. A little girl has so little idea of cause and effect, she attributes most phenomena like a melting popsicle to some kind of magic that only adults have a handle on. When she begins to see her recipes turn out the same every time she follows certain steps, and when adults supply her with explanations of why and how, she feels she is gaining some control over her destiny and is very pleased.

reading

Whenever we had a sizeable group of children, we drew picture recipes and laid them out left to right for a little pre-reading exercise. The direction was important because words on a page run from left to right and the letters within those words go from left to right. Children don't instinctively know this. They're as likely to start at the middle or end of any project as they are to begin at the beginning.

Our picture recipes featured the name of the ingredient such as "salt" and the name of the operation such as "sprinkle" and a picture of a salt shaker. Our drawings were primitive, but the children liked them because they looked much like their own work. Ruth Ingram, a very organized Berkeley nursery school teacher, used another approach. She made a file of cooking vocabulary cards with beautiful pictures of various ingredients cut out of magazines. She put the cards in clear plastic "Zip Lock" bags to protect them from spills, so they should last a long time.

Pictures serve two purposes. First, they get the children verbalizing about what they are supposed to do, and many young children need practice putting their ideas into words. Secondly, they introduce the children to symbolization. Pictures are symbols of the operation and the ingredient. The words are symbols of the same things. Indirectly, children get the idea that written words are symbols of speech, a fact not at all clear to pre-schoolers.

Our recipes which are basically simple sometimes look distressingly long because we have included a verb for practically every step. We hope it won't put off adults because it really doesn't mean more work. We chose this format to make the operations as clear as possible for children who don't instinctively know they should remove a pan from heat after its contents turn brown. By using lots of verbs as a child cooks, an adult can also take advantage of an excellent opportunity to bolster a child's vocabulary with first hand experience.

For further reading and pre-reading practice, we held up the cards from the picture recipes at the end of a cooking day and asked children what they said. After a few months, we started covering up the pictures and asking children to read the words. Even pre-schoolers could recognize the most common words like add, cut, and stir.

One further note on picture recipes. They allow children to complete recipes with minimal adult interference. Regular cooks soon learn that a picture with two spoons on it means add two spoonsful of the ingredient and so on. Self-teaching is a great help when children are constantly testing to find out how independent they really are. They also discover for themselves the value of following directions. If they go hog-wild with the salt, their own tastebuds tell them it was a bad idea.

cooking order

When deciding what recipe to do next, adults should listen to children and let their interests lead them. If children are fascinated by the bubbles the egg beater made in Eggnog, Watch-the-Bubble Pancakes could make a good follow-up project.

Trying to build on skills and use logical progression should not overshadow the fact that order comes in many forms. If, for instance, a group of children is interested in how foods grow, it's just as orderly to make recipes with foods as they come in season or to prepare holiday dishes throughout the year. For instance, the nursery class run by Zenobia Cambric and Ruth Ingram had a warm and wonderful Thanksgiving experience. Over a week, the children fixed a Thanksgiving dinner with all the trimmings which they shared with each other and their parents the day before Thanksgiving vacation. The children were very proud to see adults enjoy the cranberry-orange relish, cornmeal muffin dressing, sweet potatoes etc. they had made.

expanding lessons

An adult can inconspicuously expand all the lessons cooking offers by asking a few questions and pointing out some facts. For this reason, we've included short stories that children found interesting on each major food category. Adults can read these before children start cooking or talk about the content as they work. We've tried to touch on subjects that children frequently asked about while cooking. Adults should always encourage children to talk about how ingredients smell, feel, taste, and change and then listen attentively. This way, children learn to differentiate and sharpen all their senses.

At the end of each recipe, we've included topics of conversation designed to make the cooking experience more than an exercise in beating, grating, and measuring. With some key questions, a sensitive adult can help a child integrate what happens during cooking with the rest of his life, so the whole experience becomes more meaningful.

For instance, an adult can ask a four-year-old who has just squeezed an orange what other things he squeezes. He is usually so intent on his most recent accomplishment that he's stumped. If she can lead him around to the idea that he also squeezes his security blanket, his parents, or a favorite stuffed animal, she can build on something the child already knows and make him aware of a previously disconnected bit of knowledge.

The suggested topics are for several age levels and need to be screened for a particular child. Some will fall flat but an adult that perseveres should get a response eventually. A child who could care less about how a squash grows might take off with whether a tablespoon or one-eighth of a cup is larger.

A touch-and-feel box with various fruits and vegetables hidden behind a cover can sharpen a child's sense of touch and reinforce his knowledge of names and shapes. Storybooks are another excellent way to merge the cooking experience with the rest of a child's life. Read *"Stone Soup"* after making Alphabet Minestrone, *"The Carrot Seed"* after Carrot Cake or *"Pop Corn and Ma Goodness"* after popcorn, and the

14

impact of a cooking lesson lingers on. Older children could even make a trip to the library to get more information on questions that cooking gives rise to.

The photographs of children at work can also increase awareness and verbalization (as well as supply picture recipes of a sort). A child sees how someone his size flips, grinds, sifts, and pinches. We found the photos helped explain to children just what they were supposed to do with a spatula for instance. Because their vocabularies are small and their understanding of abstract concepts limited, children often do better with pictures than words. We found cooking operations went smoother if we prepared children the day before by looking at pictures and talking about what we were going to do.

ingredients

Ingredients provide some of cooking's most important lessons. Many four-year-olds are too sophisticated to think milk comes from cartons, but many have never seen peas in a pod, squeezed a fresh lemon, or broken open a hairy coconut. My own sister met her first uncanned green bean at 26 years of age and liked it tremendously.

So use ingredients in their natural states whenever possible. Many of our recipes call for beaten egg or chopped onion but let some of the children do the cracking, beating, and chopping beforehand, then leave an egg shell or onion top around so other kids can see where the ingredient originally came from. If you do use a processed ingredient like orange concentrate, be sure to mention what fruit it comes from and have an orange around for children to examine. Kids do not usually think in abstract terms, so they don't always make what seem like obvious connections.

While there's a place for mixes when cooking with children, it's best not to lean too heavily on them. They work out well in instances like Carrot Cake where the featured ingredients are spices, not dry ingredients. Mixes are also nice for shortening a good recipe that's too long. However, a child who uses ingredients in their most basic forms acquires an understanding of what food looks like before it's canned, frozen, dried, whipped, or concentrated and put on the grocery shelf, and this pre-packaged world makes more sense to him.

equipment

Cooking with children doesn't require expensive equipment. Most standard adult items do fine and children love to get their hands on adult tools that are usually off-limits. Let a young child switch a blender on and off or grind some peanuts in a heavy-duty meat grinder and she thinks she's one of the world's most competent people. With this in mind, take the following tips to heart only where practical.

Beaters with side handles work better with light mixtures; top handled beaters are good for heavy mixtures.

Bowls that taper to narrow bottoms work better with egg beaters. Wide-bottomed soup bowls spread the liquid too thinly.

When using egg beaters, have bowls sturdy enough to remain standing with egg beaters left in them.

Put dry ingredients like flour and sugar into bowls instead of leaving them in their sacks, to make it easier for children to measure. Kids also do better with dry ingredients using measuring cups that come in ¼, ⅓, and ½ cup sizes that they can level off at the top with their fingers.

Put honey in a squeeze bottle like the kind sold for catsup and mustard for easier measuring. Another solution—dip the measuring spoon in oil first (the disadvantage here is the oil. Oil spills are among the hardest cleanup operations).

A juicer with a wet rag underneath will not slip around so much.

Keep a towel handy for children to wipe their hands on after mixing something sticky or cracking eggs.

Many children find grating easier when the handles on the ends of the grater are bent down. This kind of grater rests fairly securely over a bowl which also catches the food. Four-sided graters are also good.

Use clear cups for measuring liquid ingredients. Draw a dark line around the cup at the correct level so children can easily see if they have the right amount.

Electrical appliances that can be moved any-where are marvelously adaptable for cooking with children. Thrift stores usually have a good selection of hot plates and meat grinders at low prices.

Muffin tins and liners are a boon to cooking with children because the size is right for one serving and the child's name can be written on the bottom of the liner to avoid mix-ups when more than one child is cooking. Children are terribly disappointed if they don't get exactly what they

17

prepared, and they have a way of remembering down to the last raisin just what the end result should have.

Put a sifter on a paper plate before adding dry ingredients. After sifting, a child can make a handy pour spout for getting the dry ingredients into the liquid mixture by bending the plate.

Children are not as likely to burn their forearms on a sideless griddle as they are on a regular frying pan. But keep a bowl of ice water handy for accidents.

Low tables or high benches and chairs for regular tables keep a small cook from tiring quickly. If he has to work at an awkward angle, he soon becomes frustrated.

A child flips more easily using two spatulas.

adapting recipes

We hope our recipes are a starting place for parents and children. Take their favorites from your collection and try to adapt them for individual servings. We discovered that many steps can be thrown out if perfection is not your aim. Don't stir until the end because children like to move along and often get stuck stirring. Leave out the ground cloves if the recipe is getting long. Be careful with pinches of this and that. If the ingredient is something like baking powder that can ruin the taste, better leave it out, because children's pinches tend to be generous.

before cooking

Perhaps the most important thing an adult can bring to cooking with children is his patience. Messes will happen. Be prepared but not afraid.

The worst instance in my memory is a three-year-old spewing pancake batter over the walls with an egg beater. Ten minutes and all was repaired. He probably never would have done it had he been given a chance to beat soapy water, outside, to his heart's content. Children generally take their efforts too seriously for sloppiness.

Never leave a potentially dangerous situation such as a frying pan or sharp knife untended by an adult. It's good to separate the cooking area from the preparation area for added safety. One adult can watch the children slicing potatoes for French fries at one table and another can monitor deep fat frying at a separate table. Low screen dividers keep excited children from accidentally knocking the cook against a hot appliance. Screens are also useful for establishing work areas and directing the flow of traffic. Avoid overcrowding the work spaces. Smooth, comfortable operations are safer.

Arrange electrical cords to eliminate any possibility of a child's tripping over them.

Try recipes beforehand with the ingredients you are going to use with children. Some flours, especially the surplus variety, require more liquid to make a good tasting muffin.

Very small children (around two) may do better making one individual serving and splitting it.

Allow plenty of time for cooking so you and the children can have a good time. Waiting lists are great for remembering whose turn it is, and they encourage children to write their own names. These lists help clear the cooking area too. An adult can tell a child hanging around and blocking progress to play at something else a while because his name will wait for him.

One new cooking operation a day is usually enough for children. Divide a recipe into two days' work if it seems like a good idea. For instance, boil and mash the sweet potatoes the day before making Sweet Potato Baskets or crack open the coconut the day before Tropical Salad.

Small children like instant results, so start with recipes like Color-Me Pudding or Celery Canoes. Later on, they are more willing to hold off for something that takes longer.

Practice play such as beating soapy water is good pre-cooking exercise. The variations are endless. Give children in a sandbox measuring equipment and some cooking utensils. Let them pour and measure rice, beans or cornmeal, and stir it up with water.

Individual recipes are especially valuable for learning how to follow directions. Group recipes are great socializing experiences and lessons in cooperation. I remember two children who usually couldn't look at each other without fighting, standing tranquilly side by side, dicing zucchini. Group projects like Tropical Salad are also excellent ice breakers for children who don't know each other.

We've indicated whether recipes are individual or group by use of identifying symbols, and perhaps a warning is in order here. Many of us got too excited about the virtues of individual recipes because the kids got so excited about what they could do all by and for themselves. But group recipes have value too.

Totally inexperienced children are not prepared for either individual or group recipes. We've put several good starting recipes at the end of the introduction. At first, few children will do every operation. An adult can step in and "take his turn" wherever good sense indicates. (But watch out for the over-protective parent who does the whole thing.)

Another pitfall to avoid is trying to cram in as many recipes as possible to keep children's interest up and build on knowledge and skills. After we calmed down, we found children loved to repeat recipes because it gave them a chance to really master skills like cracking eggs. A master egg-cracker wants to show off his expertise with endless eggnogs.

To sum up, cooking with children is fun, educational, sensual, social, constructive, and not an unreasonable burden for the ordinary parent or teacher with a hundred demands on his time. From the child's viewpoint, he shares a grown-up activity with a favorite grown up and has an added bonus of something very special to eat at the end.

crunchy bananas

(I) **you need:** ½ banana per child, sesame seeds. 1 paper cup per child, plastic knives (the kind airplanes have are perfect for children), tray for cutting banana.

peel   skin from ½ banana.

slice   into thick pieces on tray.

dip   pieces in sesame seeds. Give each child his own little cup of sesame seeds.

eat

talk about: Shape of banana slices. Other fruits we peel (avocado, potato, orange). Skins we eat. Other kinds of seeds. How many pieces child cut. How many halves in whole banana. Other ways to eat banana.

simple spaghetti

(G) **you need:** Spaghetti, tomato sauce, water, grated cheese (optional). Kettle (electric works well because it can be moved low enough for group of children to watch) or large electric frying pan, slotted spoon, measuring spoon.

break   spaghetti strands into boiling water.

cook   until spaghetti is soft (adult tests sample strands).

lift   out with slotted spoon and put on plate.

add   1 tablespoon tomato sauce.

add   little grated cheese.

stir

talk about: What happens to spaghetti after cooking. Other foods that get soft with cooking (potatoes, carrots). Foods that harden with cooking (eggs). What boiling means.

play dough

Deceptively simple. Small children usually need help stirring, but they love coloring and kneading. Good way to learn colors.

(1) **you need:** Flour, salt, warm water, food coloring, oil. Bowl, spoon for stirring, measuring cups and spoon.

measure	½ cup flour into bowl.
add	¼ cup salt.
measure	¼ cup warm water in 1-cup measuring cup.
add	food coloring to water.
stir	
add	water-food coloring mixture to dry ingredients.
stir	
add	½ teaspoon oil.
stir	again.
knead	on floured tray until smooth. Add just enough flour to keep dough from sticking. Then use as clay. Store in plastic bag in refrigerator.

talk about: Other things we knead. Favorite color. Dry ingredients vs. wet ingredients. Different texture of flour and salt. What other food salt resembles (children often think it's sugar).

color-me pudding

Good first project. Delicious way for young children to learn colors.

(1) **you need:** Instant vanilla pudding mix, ice cold milk, food coloring. Paper cups, plastic spoons, measuring cup and spoon.

measure	1 tablespoon instant pudding into paper cup.
add	¼ cup ice cold milk.
stir	with plastic spoon until mix dissolves and pudding thickens.
add	food coloring.
stir	

talk about: Child's favorite color. Names of other colors. What happens to pudding mix (dissolves). What happens to mixture (thickens). Which is bigger, ¼ cup or 1 tablespoon.

25

great grated potatoes

① ***you need:*** Fat for frying, potatoes, salt. Flat grater with ends bent so it remains stable when placed over plate, frying pan, spatula, forks, plates.

grate   potato onto plate. If working with group, station one child on each side of table.

carry   plate with grated potato to frying pan.

place   potatoes in one of four corners of frying pan. Adult may have to do this first time, all the while talking about the need to be careful around hot equipment.

flip   after bottom brown.

lift   out of pan and place on same plate potatoes were grated onto (adult job at first).

sprinkle   with salt.

talk about: Change in color after cooking. Other foods we fry. What made potatoes turn brown. Other foods we grate (cabbage, cheese). Other ways to eat potatoes.

color-me frosting

(1) **you need:** Powdered sugar, milk, flavoring (vanilla, mint, lemon etc.), food coloring, graham cracker. Small paper cups, wooden ice cream spoons or throat sticks, measuring spoons.

measure   2 heaping tablespoons powdered sugar into small cup.

add   1 teaspoon milk.

add   1 drop flavoring (put flavoring in squeeze bottles — empty food coloring bottles work well — or have child first put 1 drop in spoon to avoid having too much flavoring get in frosting).

add   1 drop food coloring.

stir   with wooden spoon (mixture will be runny but easy for beginners to work with).

spread   with spoon on graham cracker.

talk about: Names of colors. Smells of flavorings. Which ingredients are dry, which wet. Which is bigger, tablespoon or teaspoon. Other foods with vanilla flavor. Other kinds of sugar. Favorite colors.

27

popcorn

Ⓖ ***you need:*** Popcorn, oil, salt, butter (optional). Electric popper with glass top.

pour	enough oil in popper to cover bottom well, about 3 tablespoons.
test	kernel every few minutes. When kernel pops, oil is right temperature.
add	enough popcorn to cover bottom.
place	top on.
shake	occasionally.
wait	for kernels to stop popping.
pour	into individual cups.
sprinkle	with salt.

talk about: Other kinds of corn. Why popcorn pops (see introduction). Noise popcorn makes. Other things that explode. First person to hear popping kernel. Other seeds we eat (peanuts).

lumpia
(phillipine pancakes)

Ⓖ ***you need:*** Flour, water, seasoned meat and vegetable mixture, oil. The meat/vegetable mixture can be made with just about any combination of vegetables and ground beef. Vary the proportion of meat to vegetables according to what's available. Pastry brush, electric frying pan with sides, basket to hold lumpias while deep fat frying, tablespoon.

Children can watch as adult makes lumpias. Mix 2 tablespoons flour and three tablespoons water for each lumpia. Figure 1 lumpia per child and increase proportions accordingly. Pour about ¼ cup lumpia mixture onto hot greased griddle, and brush it out with a pastry brush to make a circle about 5 inches across. Flip to cook both sides. After enough lumpias are made, fill the pan with oil for deep fat frying.

place	1 tablespoon seasoned meat/vegetable mixture in center of lumpia.
fold	both sides over mixture.
fold	bottom over sides and top over bottom to make square envelope.
place	in frying basket.
fry	(adult job)
remove	from basket with tongs.
drain	on paper towel.

talk about: Shape of pancake (circle), of finished lumpia (square). Other things we fold (paper, clothes in drawer, sheets). Other things we put in envelopes. Where the Phillipine Islands are and what language is spoken there.

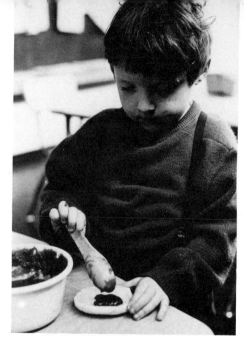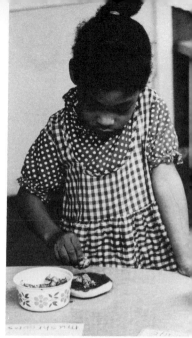

easiest pizza ever

① *you need:* Refrigerated biscuits, tomato sauce, thin cheese slices cut into 1″ squares, slice of salami. Small rolling pin or cylinder from block set, measuring spoon, oven, tray for rolling, cookie sheet.

roll	out 1 refrigerated biscuit with rolling pin or cylindrical block.
spread	with 1 tablespoon tomato sauce.
place	1 slice salami over sauce.
top	with slice of cheese.
place	on cookie sheet.
bake	about 6 minutes at 475°.

talk about: What happens to cheese. Other foods that melt. What made cheese melt. Spiciest ingredient. Other things to put on pizza.

milk shake it yourself

① **you need:** Ice cream (kids love a choice of flavors), milk. Jar with tight fitting lid (such as peanut butter, jelly, or soft margarine containers), cups, straws, measuring cups.

scoop   ¼ cup ice cream with cup that levels off at top with exact amount. Leave ice cream out ahead of time to make scooping easier.

drop   into jar with tight fitting lid.

add   ¼ cup milk.

screw   on top tightly.

shake   with both hands until the mixture is the right consistency (children have strong—and differing—opinions on this).

pour   into cup.

drink   with straw.

Note—This recipe can be dressed up with syrup and flavorings after children have the basic steps down.

talk about: What happens to ice cream. Favorite flavors. Number of shakes child gave his milkshake. Who can shake his hand, foot, head, body etc. (Hokey Pokey song is a good follow-up to milk shakes.) How to tell where the recipe begins.

31

Stone Soup tonight

needs Salt

Cabbage is nice –

too bad we don't have potatoes

I like mushrooms

I had some once with

carrots

beans

pepper

barley

turnips

nice of you to share

and I saw it with my own eyes

Amazingly good too

welcome

32

stone soup

(G) This recipe really touches small children's sense of humor. Be sure to read or tell *Stone Soup* several times beforehand (Marcia Brown, *Stone Soup, An Old Tale Retold*, [New York: Charles Scribner's Sons, 1947]).* Ask each child to bring in something for soup. A few will probably bring in stones but in case not, have a few well scrubbed stones on hand to put in the pot. Help children wash and cut whatever they bring in. Make enough broth from dry soup powder to cook vegetables. Throw in some rice or noodles at the end.

*Three hungry soldiers are marching toward a French village. Word that they are on their way goes before them and the peasants hide their food, knowing soldiers are always hungry. When the soldiers ask for a bite, everyone in the village replies, "I have no food." But the clever soldiers have a plan. They announce that they are making stone soup and carefully put three big stones in a kettle of water. The villagers are fascinated. When one soldier says sadly how much better the soup would be with a little salt and pepper, a boy runs to get some. "A good stone soup should have cabbage too," another soldier says, and a woman finds a cabbage or two. And so it goes until the peasants have opened their cupboards. Finally, when the soup is done, the soldiers and villagers pronounce it fit for a king, and everyone feasts, drinks, and dances far into the night. Next morning when the soldiers have to leave, the peasants thank them for teaching them how to make stone soup. "We shall never go hungry now that we know," they proclaim.

talk about: Number of different kinds of vegetables children brought in. Favorite vegetables, soups. Which vegetables need their skins taken off. What cooking does to vegetables.

33

fruits

Almost everyone has a favorite fruit. Next to honey, a bear loves berries. Birds often fill up on figs and peaches. Certain worms like apples better than anything.

In the Spring, fruit flowers blossom on trees and plants and vines. Inside each blossom are a stamen and a pistil. This pistil doesn't shoot. It is the girl part of the plant and deep inside it is the beginning of a seed. When powdery pollen from the boy part, the stamen, is sprinkled over the pistil, it works its way down to the tiny beginning of a seed and fertilizes it.

A fertilized fruit blossom starts changing right away. A seed forms and a fruit grows around the seed to protect it and to provide food for it. The fruit even helps the seed get to a good place to grow into a bush, tree, or vine. Birds carry good tasting fruits away from the mother tree. Birds eat the fruit and drop the seed. Sometimes they drop it in a good place and a new fruit plant grows.

People eat fruits and throw away the seed but that's fine. The world would soon fill up with cherries, pears, peaches, apples, berries, plums and grapes if every seed grew into new fruit trees and plants and vines.

fruit jello for everybody

good for beginners

(G) *An early explorer from across the ocean brought banana plants with him when he sailed over to the land of the Indians. He gave plants out for presents and the steamy jungle where his new friends lived was perfect for bananas. Indians started roasting green ones and eating them like bread. Sometimes they boiled them for a vegetable. They even dried them to eat like raisins.*

you need: Large package fruit gelatin, can pineapple slices, 2 bananas, hot water. Measuring cup and spoon, whisk for stirring, kitchen knife, pan.

measure	1 cup of fruit gelatin.
pour	4 cups hot water into pan.
add	gelatin.
stir	until gelatin dissolves.
chill	until gelatin is slightly set.
slice	2 bananas.
cut	pineapple slices into bite-sized pieces.
mix	into gelatin.
chill	until firm.

talk about: Change in texture. What happened to gelatin powder. Other foods that dissolve. Other liquids that turn solid when cold.

cool shake

① **you need:** Chopped ice (beforehand, have some energetic children put ice cubes in plastic bags and pound the bags with small hammers. If each child wants to do his own, use plastic sandwich bags and about 2 ice cubes per child), sweet fruit juice like apricot nectar or pineapple, powdered milk. Jar with tight-fitting lid such as peanut butter, jelly, or soft margarine containers, cups, straws, measuring spoons and cup.

measure	¼ cup chopped ice into jar with tight-fitting lid.
add	3 tablespoons powdered milk.
add	4 tablespoons sweet fruit juice.
screw	on top of jar (or snap on if plastic container).
shake	until powdered milk dissolves.

talk about: What happens to powdered milk. Other ways milk comes. How to get juice out of fruits (squeeze). All names of fruit child can think of. What makes shake cold. Another way that water comes (try to get at liquid with small children; older kids might know about steam too).

lemonade

(1) *Long ago, sailors fell sick from a disease called scurvy when they made long sea voyages. Scurvy gave sailors sore gums and sleepy heads. One day, a clever doctor noticed that sailors who ate lemons did not get scurvy. "Lemons are the answer," he said. It was the vitamin C in lemons that did the job.*

you need: one-half lemon per child, sugar, water, ice cubes. Measuring cup and spoons, squeezer, sharp knife, long-handled spoon.

cut	1 lemon in half.
squeeze	out juice from one-half lemon (anchor squeezer with wet rag).
pour	juice into glass.
add	2 teaspoons sugar (vary according to size and tartness of lemon).
add	½ cup water.
stir	until sugar dissolves.
add	2 ice cubes.

talk about: What makes lemonade tart, sweet. What ice cubes do. How many pieces child has after cutting lemon in half. How many pieces in whole lemon. What lemons grow on. Other fruits with lots of juice. Other tart tasting foods. Other things we squeeze (people, teddy bears, animals). What dissolve means. Difference between ice cubes and water.

37

banana bread

Bananas are picked when they are absolutely green with not a speck of yellow. Then they ripen in the sun until they taste good.

(1) **you need:** Beaten egg, oil, sugar, ¼ small ripe banana per child, baking powder, flour. Bowl, spoon for stirring, measuring spoons, paper plate, muffin tin, liners, sifter, oven.

measure	1 tablespoon egg into bowl.
add	1 tablespoon oil.
stir	
mash	¼ small banana with liquids.
stir	again.
measure	¼ cup flour into sifter.
add	⅛ teaspoon baking powder.
add	⅛ cup sugar.
sift	onto paper plate, then add to liquid mixture.
stir	
pour	into lined muffin tin.
bake	in 350° oven until done, about 15 minutes.

talk about: How bananas grow. Other desserts with bananas. How to tell when banana is ripe. Color of bananas when picked (green). What ripens fruit (sunshine helps). Strong smell of bananas. How unripe bananas taste. What black spots on bananas mean. Which ingredient made bread light. Change from liquid to solid after cooking. Other kinds of bread. How many quarters in 1 whole banana.

blueberry muffin

Blueberries grow on bushes that have a grayish powder on them. We eat blueberry seeds along with the berry but hardly notice them because they are so small.

(1) **you need:** Flour, salt, baking powder, sugar, beaten egg, milk, blueberries. Measuring spoons, bowl, spoon for stiring, egg beater, muffin tin, liners, sifter, paper plate.

measure	2 teaspoons beaten egg into bowl.
add	1 tablespoon milk.
beat	with egg beater.
measure	3 tablespoons flour into sifter.
add	pinch salt.
add	¼ teaspoon baking powder.
add	2 teaspoons sugar.
sift	onto paper plate, then add to liquid mixture.
add	14 blueberries
stir	
spoon into	lined muffin tin.
bake	350° oven until top firm, about 15 minutes.

talk about: How berries grow. Other kinds of berries. Other kinds of muffins. How many quarter teaspoons in 1 teaspoon. Wet ingredients vs. dry ingredients. Change in texture of batter after cooking. A number more than 14. A number less than 14. Other ways to eat blueberries.

tropical fruit salad

Farmers start new pineapple plants from the leafy hat on top of the pineapple. Roots grow out the bottom and a plant shoots out the top. Pineapples and coconuts both like hot rainy weather.

(G) **you need:** Small pineapple, cantaloupe, strawberries, coconut,* peach, powdered sugar. Sharp knife for cutting pineapple, kitchen knives for cutting other fruits, melon baller, grater, nail, hammer, utensils for tossing.

cut	small pineapple into ½ inch slices (adult job).
trim	off skin.
cut	into bite-sized chunks from around core.
scoop	melon balls from cantaloupe or other melon.
hull	basket strawberries.
slice	strawberries.
*pound	nail into two places on coconut.
*drain	out milk.
*drop	coconut from high place or pound with hammer to break open.
*pull	coconut meat away from skin. Skin comes away easily if coconut is heated 30 minutes in 350° oven.
grate	about 1 cup coconut or until workers wear out.
slice	1 fresh peach.
sprinkle	fruit with a little powdered sugar.
toss	

talk about: favorite fruit, taste of fresh pineapple juice, coconut milk. Sound of coconut milk swooshing around. Shapes of cut pineapple (usually triangular vs. melon balls). Clingstone or freestone peach.

*Coconut can be done the day before. It's exciting enough to stand alone.

baked apple

① *you need:* 1 apple per child, brown sugar or cinnamon candies, cinnamon, nutmeg. Knife or apple corer, small pie tin, measuring spoons, spoon for basting, oven.

wash   apple.

cut   slice off bottom so apple rests securely on cutting surface.

ream   out core with apple corer or knife (corer works best for small children).

place   apple in small pie tin.

fill   core with brown sugar or cinnamon candies. A funnel made from a piece of stiff paper helps children get the sugar into the small hole.

sprinkle   with cinnamon and nutmeg.

add   1 tablespoon water to pan.

bake   in 350° oven about 30 minutes, until apple is tender.

baste   juices over apple occasionally.

talk about: What cooking does to apple. Which ingredient sweetens. Where nutmeg and cinnamon come from. Other desserts that have nutmeg and cinnamon. Number of seeds in core. Where apple was attached to tree.

apple toast

In spring, the codling moth lays her eggs on apple tree leaves and twigs because she knows the baby caterpillars that hatch out will want to eat an apple.

(1) ***you need:*** ¼ medium apple per child, butter, sugar, cinnamon, bread. Parer, knife for slicing, knife for buttering, measuring spoons, spatula, cookie sheet, oven.

peel	¼ medium apple.
slice	apple.
butter	slice of bread.
place	apple slices on bread.
sprinkle	½ teaspoon sugar over top.
sprinkle	little cinnamon over sugar.
place	on cookie sheet with spatula (on top of paper towel with child's name on it).
bake	about 15 minutes in 375° oven.

talk about: Change in apple's texture after cooking. Which ingredient made toast sweet. Which ingredient is a spice. How apples grow. How many quarters in one apple. How many slices child got from apple quarter. Other kinds of toast. Other ways of eating apple.

apple chunklets

(1) **you need:** Apple (one medium per child), honey, cinnamon. Parer, bowl, grinder with medium attachment, spoon for stirring.

pare   1 apple. Don't worry if child misses some skin. Taste doesn't suffer. For beginners, paring is easier if adult holds apple while child wields parer.

cut   apple into large chunks, removing seeds and core.

grind   apple into small bowl. Use attachment with medium holes.

add   squirt of honey. For easy dispensing, put honey in a catsup-style squeeze bottle.

sprinkle   heavily with cinnamon.

stir

talk about: Other things we grind (teeth, meat for hamburger). Change in texture after grinding. Which ingredient sweetens mixture. Which ingredient is a spice. Where seeds are located. Where apples were attached to tree. Different kinds of apples. Other ways we eat them. Other fruits with cores (pears). Number of seeds in core.

fresh fruit frappe

Look closely and you'll see the many, many little fruits that make up one strawberry. Each little fruit has one seed.

① you need: ½ orange per child, ¼ banana per child, ice cream, vanilla, 1 strawberry per child, milk. Blender, measuring spoons and cup, ice cream scooper, knife for cutting, juicer, glass, straws.

squeeze	½ orange. Anchor juicer with wet rag underneath.
pour	juice into blender.
add	¼ banana.
add	1 strawberry.
add	¼ teaspoon vanilla.
add	⅛ cup milk.
add	scoop ice cream.
blend	until smooth.
pour	into glass.

talk about: Which is bigger, ⅛ cup or ¼ teaspoon. How different fruits grow. What color drink will be after blending. What blending does (makes hard foods soft). Other flavors of shakes. How many halves in 1 orange. Other things we squeeze (teddy bears, parents, friends).

blueberry crisp

What color are blueberries?

(1) ***you need:*** Blueberries, flour, sugar, baking powder, salt, cinnamon, beaten egg, melted butter or margarine. Bowl, spoon for stirring, measuring spoons, muffin tin, liner, oven, egg beater, sifter.

put	20 blueberries in lined muffin tin.
measure	1 teaspoon beaten egg into bowl.
add	2 teaspoons melted margarine or butter.
beat	with egg beater.
measure	2 tablespoons flour into sifter over paper plate.
add	1½ teaspoons sugar.
add	⅛ teaspoon baking powder.
pinch	salt.
sprinkle	cinnamon.
sift	onto paper plate. Then add to liquid mixture.
stir	
spoon	on top of berries.
bake	in 375° oven until top is crisp, about 12 minutes.

talk about: How berries grow. Other kinds of berries. Other ways to eat berries. What crisp means. Why recipe called Blueberry Crisp. Other crisp foods we eat (carrots, celery). Opposite of crisp (soggy).

hot applesauce

Johnny Appleseed was a man who lived in the United States when it was full of pioneers but not many apple trees. He walked around the country planting apple seeds wherever the soil looked right. He knew children love apples.

① ***you need:*** 1 apple per child, brown sugar, water, cinnamon. Parer, knife, measuring spoons, long wooden spoon for stirring, frying pan, heat source, plate, forks or spoons, bowl.

peel	apple.
slice	apple into small pieces.
mix	with 3 tablespoons water in bowl.
add	1 tablespoon brown sugar.
sprinkle	cinnamon.
stir	
pour	into medium-hot frying pan.
stir	with wooden spoon until apple is soft, about 10 minutes (depends on size of pieces).
cool	a little and eat.

talk about: How apples grow. Other fruits that grow on trees. Different colors that apples come in. Other foods we peel. Number of seeds in core. Change in apple's texture after cooking. Other foods that get soft after cooking (potatoes, carrots). Foods that get hard after cooking (eggs, bread dough). Other foods with cinnamon.

peanut butter

You can call peanuts goober peas if you'd rather. Peanuts are the seed of the peanut plant.

(1) *you need:* Seven peanuts in their shells per child (plus many extras for eating), peanut oil, salt, crackers. Sturdy grinder with fine attachment, measuring spoon, small spoon for stirring, small hammers for breaking shells (optional but fun).

pick	7 peanuts and put in small cup.
shell	peanuts. Have another cup for shelled peanuts.
pour	peanuts into grinder. Place towel or potholder between grinder and table for secure fit.
add	1 teaspoon peanut oil.
grind	peanuts into cup.
sprinkle	little salt into ground nuts.
stir	
spread	on crackers.

talk about: Other nuts we eat. Other seeds we eat. How many peanuts in each shell. Ways to eat peanut butter. Beginnings of new peanut plant (split peanut in two and look for tiny cotyledon at bottom of one of the halves). Purpose of peanut shell (to protect seed).

48

crunchy
salad

① **you need:** ¼ apple per child, 2″ celery, mayonnaise, raisins, 4 peanuts per child. Parer, knife for cutting, measuring spoons, spoon for stirring, bowl, bowl for peanut shells, ruler.

pare	¼ apple.
cut	apple into small pieces.
measure	2″ from stalk of celery.
cut	celery into small pieces.
add	1 tablespoon mayonnaise.
add	7 raisins.
shell	4 salted peanuts.
split	peanuts into halves and add to other ingredients.
stir	

talk about: How many inches in whole stalk of celery. How many peanuts in one shell. How many halves in 1 peanut. Sweetest ingredient (raisins). How many inches child is. What holds salad together. Names of crunchy ingredients. Other kinds of salad.

orange ceasar

Years back, farmers burned smudge pots filled with hay, damp leaves, and whatever else they could find to keep their orange trees warm in cold weather. Smudge pots sent up huge clouds of stinky smoke that held in the heat just like walls hold the heat inside a house.

(G) *you need:* Plain yogurt, orange yogurt, oranges, coconut (fresh or packaged),* honey. Measuring cup and spoons, squeezer, sharp knife, grater, blender, hammer, nail.

measure	1 cup plain yogurt into blender.
add	1 cup orange yogurt.
cut	3 juice oranges in half.
squeeze	enough juice to measure 1 cup. Wet rag underneath squeezer anchors it to the spot.
pour	juice into blender.
*break	open fresh coconut and drain out milk.
peel	meat away from skin. Easy job if coconut is warmed in 350° oven for 30 minutes.
grate	2 tablespoons coconut. Put in blender.
add	2 tablespoons honey or sugar.
blend	until smooth.
chill	about 1 hour.
blend	again just before serving.

talk about: How oranges and coconuts grow. Taste of coconut milk. Which ingredients are dairy foods. Which ingredient sweetens. Other fruits we squeeze. Where coconuts grow. How many pieces child has after cutting orange in half.

*If using fresh coconut, consider opening and grating it day before.

gelatin magic

Grapes are one of the oldest fruits that people have grown for food. Raisins are a certain kind of grape that's dried by the sun or by machines.

① **you need:** Fruit juice such as grape, apple, orange (not pineapple), unflavored gelatin, ice cubes. Measuring cup, measuring spoons, spoon for stirring, saucepan, hot plate or other heat source, paper cup, tray or bowl for holding ice water.

measure	½ cup juice into small saucepan.
add	2 teaspoons unflavored gelatin.
stir	over low heat until gelatin dissolves.
pour	mixture into paper cup.
add	1 ice cube.
place	cup in tray or bowl of ice water.
stir	occasionally until mixture hardens, about 10 minutes — depends on how cold the water is. When it starts, it goes quickly.

talk about: How mixture changed from liquid to solid. How many half cups in a whole cup (have some water on hand to demonstrate). What happens to gelatin, ice cube. Other things that harden when chilled (ice cream, water, candy bars, mud puddles). What makes mixture harden (gelatin, a special food substance that can soak up lots of liquid). Something else that soaks up liquid (sponge). Where gelatin comes from (it's a protein that comes out of bones after they are boiled for a while).

51

vegetables

Vegetables come from all different places on vegetable plants. Peas are the seeds of the pea plant and carrots are the roots of carrot plants. We eat lettuce leaves, celery stems and the flowers of cauliflower and artichoke plants.

All these vegetables need food while they grow but they don't eat scrambled eggs or fried chicken like people. Their roots absorb minerals and water from the ground. Their stems carry the minerals and water from the roots up to the leaves, and the leaves, with the help of the sun, turn the minerals and water into food for the plants to grow on.

Did you ever break the stem of a plant and feel something watery? That stem was probably carrying food and water. When leaves don't make food anymore and the roots are not getting water and minerals from the ground, the stems dry up. Some stems, like cactus stems, hold water for a long time even if no rain falls. Many a thirsty traveler with a dry canteen has said, "Hooray for cactus," after sucking a cactus stem.

fresh vegetable dip

for harvest time

Cucumbers are the fleshy fruits that grow off the trailing cucumber vine. We usually eat the big ones raw. Little ones, called pickling cukes, make pickles.

Ⓖ **you need:** Almost any assortment of fresh vegetables: cauliflower, peppers, zucchini, cucumbers, celery, tomatoes, dip (see Delicious Dressing). Water, towels, knives, trays for cutting.

wash	vegetables.
dry	gently with towels.
cut	flowers from cauliflower.
slice	celery into 2 or 3 inch lengths.
slice	cucumbers into thick rounds.
slice	zucchini into sticks or rounds. Let children choose the shapes as much as possible.
cut	tomatoes into fat wedges.
arrange	on tray.
dip	into favorite dip. See Delicious Dressing.

talk about: Geometric shapes of vegetables. What parts of plants different vegetables are. Other ways of eating vegetables. Which vegetables child has seen growing. Other things we dip (toes in bathtub to test water).

53

barbecued corn

Pollen from the flowers at the top of a corn stalk drops down to the stringy silks peeking out of the corn husk. Female flowers are hiding inside the husk at the other end of the silks. The pollen travels down the silk tube and fertilizes the female flowers. Each fertilized flower turns into a kernel of corn which is the seed of the corn plant.

(G) *you need:* 1 ear corn per child, butter, salt, pepper. Newspaper, water, charcoal for fire, tongs, aluminum foil, pie plate.

beforehand: start charcoal fire.

husk	corn.
remove	silks. Don't worry about getting them all.
wet	newspaper.
wrap	ear in wet newspaper.
wrap	in foil, shiny side out.
put	in glowing coals. (Start fire at least ½ hour before.)
turn	several times with tongs as corn cooks.
remove	in about 10 minutes. Depends on heat of fire.
remove	foil and paper.
butter	Easy way for children to butter: melt butter and pour into pie tin. Let children roll ears of corn in pan.
sprinkle	with salt and pepper.
eat	

talk about: Texture of silks. Role of silks in pollination. What part of plant corn kernels are. Why corn cobs are called ears (because they look like ears hanging off stalk). Other kinds of corn (popcorn). What happens to butter.

halloween custard

A pumpkin is a member of the squash family, and it grows on a long, trailing vine like other squashes. If you stepped on a pumpkin, you would squash a squash.

① *you need:* Beaten egg, milk, vanilla, canned pumpkin, brown sugar, cinnamon. Measuring spoons, spoon for stirring, bowl, egg beater, muffin tin, liner, large pan of water to cook custard in, oven.

measure 1 tablespoon beaten egg into bowl with narrow bottom.

add 2 tablespoons milk.

add ¼ teaspoon vanilla.

add 1 tablespoon pumpkin.

add 1 teaspoon brown sugar.

sprinkle cinnamon.

beat with egg beater until bubbly.

pour into lined muffin tin. Set muffin tin in pan of water about ½ to 1″ deep.

bake in 350° oven for about 30 minutes.

talk about: Texture of custard (many children are very suspicious of it at first). Other squashes. What time of year we eat a lot of pumpkin. What's inside a pumpkin. Another orange vegetable (sweet potatoes, carrots). How cooking changed mixture from liquid to solid. How cold can also change liquids to solid (example: ice cubes, popsicles). Where cinnamon comes from. Delicious smell from oven. Other kinds of sugar.

56

corn fritters

(1) **you need:** Bisquick, milk, corn, beaten egg, grease for frying pan, salt. Measuring spoons, spoon for stirring, bowl, 2 spatulas, electric skillet.

measure 2 tablespoons Bisquick into bowl.

add 1 teaspoon corn (either drained canned corn or corn scraped off the ear).

add 1 tablespoon milk.

add 1 teaspoon beaten egg.

mix

drop two spoonsful of batter into greased and heated frying pan.

flip when brown.

remove to plate.

sprinkle with salt.

talk about: How corn grows (it's helpful to have an ear of corn around). Other ways to eat corn. Change in dough after cooking. What made bottom of fritter brown. Other foods we fry and flip. Which ingredient is a dairy food, a vegetable. Number of ingredients. Which is bigger, tablespoon or teaspoon. How to tell where to begin recipe.

alphabet minestrone

Tomatoes are fruit of the tomato plant. Indians grew tomatoes long before anybody else knew about them. A few brave explorers tried tomatoes when they sailed across the ocean to the land of the Indians. "Yummy," they cried and brought them back for their countrymen who were afraid to eat them for years.

Ⓖ ***you need:*** Beefstock base, salt, two green onions, garlic bulb, tomato paste, carrot, celery, green beans (about 16), parsley, basil, dill, marjoram, rosemary, thyme, tarragon, dill, (assortment of fresh and dried), pea pods, zucchini, spinach, alphabet noodles, parmesan cheese. Kettle, long-handled spoon for stirring, knives, garlic press, parer, hand chopper, wooden bowl for chopping, grater for cheese, measuring cups and spoons.

measure	10 cups water into large kettle. Add more water whenever soup gets too thick.
add	6 tablespoons or 7 envelopes beefstock base.
add	2 teaspoons salt.
cut	2 green onions with scissors or knife and add.
peel	2 cloves garlic.
squeeze	into kettle with garlic press.
add	3 tablespoons tomato paste.
simmer	about 15 minutes.
pare	1 carrot.
dice	carrot.
dice	1 stalk celery.
cut	16 fresh green beans into 1″ pieces. Have ends already snipped off. Too many piles confuse children.
add	to broth and simmer about 30 minutes.
cut	1 tablespoon fresh parsley, 2 large leaves fresh basil or other herb with scissors. Try to have a few fresh seasonings. Use ⅓ quantity for dried herbs and spices.

58

add	⅛ teaspoon ground marjoram, rosemary, thyme, tarragon, dill.
stir	into broth.
shell	about 40 pea pods. Let children count as high as they can.
dice	2 zucchini.
tear	bunch spinach after removing bottom part of stems.
add	to broth.
cook	20 to 30 minutes until vegetables almost tender.
add	1 cup alphabet noodles. Let children find their initials and put in handful.
grate	1 cup parmesan cheese. For younger children, have cheese already grated and let them measure.
add	cheese when noodles done.

talk about: Favorite vegetables. Where different vegetables come from. What parts of plants different vegetables come from. Favorite cooking operation. Which vegetable comes already packaged (peas). Which belongs to squash family (zucchini). Which vegetable is a root (carrot), a bulb (onion, garlic), a leaf (spinach), a fruit (zucchini), seed (pea), a pod (bean). Changes in textures of vegetables after cooking. Other kinds of soup. How boiling soup looks. Vegetable skins we don't eat.

59

celery canoes

a favorite of the very young

We eat the stems of celery plants and use the seeds for flavoring other foods.

(1) **you need:** celery, peanut butter, cheese spread (see below). Knife for cutting, butter knife for spreading, water for washing, towels for drying.

wash
dry　　　bunch of celery.

tear　　　stalks off.

cut　　　or break into 3 inch pieces.

spread　　　with peanut butter or room temperature cheese spread. Use commercial variety or recipe below.

cheese spread

(for older children to make)

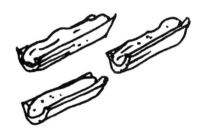

you need: Cream cheese, cheddar cheese, green onions or chives, Worcestershire sauce. Bowl, measuring spoons, spoon for stirring, scissors.

cream　　　about 3 ounces softened cream cheese in small bowl.

grate　　　2 or 3 tablespoons cheddar cheese and add to cream cheese.

cut　　　1 green onion top with scissors and add.

add　　　dash Worcestershire sauce.

mix

talk about: Another vegetable with a stalk (corn). The leaves of celery plant. What part of celery we eat. Function of stem. Other green vegetables. How noisy celery is to eat. Other noisy foods.

60

artichokes

We eat the flower bud of the artichoke plant. If a farmer does not pick the bud quickly, it grows into a flower—beautiful to look at but yucky to eat.

you need: One small artichoke per child, oil, vinegar or lemon peel, garlic cloves (½ per artichoke), dip. Pot with cover, sharp knife, fork, bowl for used leaves, heat source, measuring spoons.

fill	pot with water.
add	about ½ teaspoon oil per artichoke.
add	couple dashes vinegar or lemon peel.
add	½ clove garlic per artichoke.
cut	stem off bottom of small artichokes.
add	to water.
heat	to boiling.
cover	
simmer	until leaves come off easily and stem is tender, about 20 minutes.
dip	in mayonnaise, lemon-butter, or other dip.
scrape	off bottom leaves with teeth. Discard rest of leaves. Let children find the heart. Help them scrape off the thistly choke with spoon. Assure them it's good to eat.

talk about: What part of the artichoke plant we eat. Where flower petals are. Why artichoke didn't turn into a pretty flower. Other flowers we eat (cauliflower, broccoli). Other foods we dip.

grow your own bean sprouts

(G) ***you need:*** Mung beans, alfalfa beans, lentils, or raw sunflower seeds,* large size baby food jars (actually for junior foods), fine plastic screening (available at hardware stores), rubber bands, tape, measuring spoons. Grow two or three different kinds of beans at the same time so children can compare. Or grow something really different like an onion.

day 1

Write name on tape and stick tape on large-size baby food jar. Children feel strongly about just whose beans are whose. Measure two teaspoons beans into jar. Put squares of fine plastic screening over top of jar and secure with rubber band. Cut squares about one inch wider than top of jar. Pour room temperature water through screen until jar is full. (Put jar in large pan of some kind to catch water that spills as child pours.) Let beans soak overnight but not more than 12 hours in a dark, warm place. Stand jars upright.

day 2

Drain water from beans. Pour room temperature water over beans and swirl water and beans around jar for a minute. Turn jar over and drain water through screen. Beans should be rinsed and drained twice a day although once is usually enough to prevent mold from setting in and to encourage growth. In hot, dry climates, two rinsings and drainings a day are a must. If children are eager, let them rinse and drain several times a day. Their efforts will speed growth. Set jars on sides.

62

day 3	Same procedure as day 2.
day 4	Same procedure as day 2. Some beans will have sprouted.
day 5	Same procedure as day 2. Beans are now ready to eat. Make an Egg Foo Yung! Or sprinkle sprouts in a peanut butter sandwich. At nursery school, the children enjoyed cooking sprouts (grown by teacher the previous week) during the week that theirs were growing and taking their sprouts home to share with their families.

talk about: Tiny shoots that sprout from beans. What sprouts use for food. Difference between sprouts and roots (one goes above the ground when planted and the other goes below ground). Other seeds we eat (corn, peanuts, peas). What mung beans need before they sprout (try to lead conversation to moisture, heat). Other kinds of beans.

*Eat sunflower seeds on third day. They taste a little odd after that.

63

sweet potato baskets

The inside of a real sweet potato is yellow and dry. If it looks like a sweet potato but the inside is orange and moist, it is probably a yam.

(1) **you need:** Mashed sweet potatoes, oranges (one-half per child), brown sugar, butter, marshmallows (small), cinnamon, nutmeg. Squeezer, wet rag to anchor squeezer, spoon for stirring, grater, knife to cut orange, measuring cups and spoons, bowl.

before: Peel, cook, and mash sweet potatoes.

cut	1 orange in half.
grate	small amount of peel and shake into bowl.
squeeze	orange half and save shell.
pour	juice into bowl with peel.
add	¼ cup mashed sweet potatoes. Use measuring cup that levels off on top or the job will get too sticky.
add	1 tablespoon brown sugar.
sprinkle	with cinnamon and nutmeg.
stir	
pile	into orange half.
top	with 4 or 5 small marshmallows, maybe one for each year of child's age.
brown	for 10 or 15 minutes in 400° oven.

talk about: Smell of orange peel. Why marshmallows melted. How squeezer forced out all the juice. What part of plant sweet potato is. Other roots we eat. Other materials that melt (snow, butter, ice cubes). How many halves in a whole. How many quarters in a whole. Other fruits with lots of juice. Eye of sweet potato that could be the start of another sweet potato plant.

suggestion: Grow sweet potato vine. Suspend half a sweet potato on toothpicks in a glass of water, cut side down. Vine grows quickly.

65

refried beans

ⓖ you need: Bacon fat, clove garlic, flour tortillas, cumin, pinto beans. Kettle for boiling beans, masher, garlic press, long-handled wooden spoon, strainer, bowl, heat source.

before: cover 2 cups dry pinto beans with water and let soak overnight.

drain	beans in strainer.
put	beans in pot.
cover	with fresh water.
simmer	until tender, 2 to 3 hours.
mash	beans with masher.
add	2 tablespoons bacon fat.
peel	1 clove garlic.
squeeze	into beans using garlic press.
add	1 teaspoon cumin.
stir	with long-handled wooden spoon.
heat	for about 10 minutes in pot.
put	1 tablespoon refried beans along center of quartered flour torilla.
fold	tortilla quarter to make sandwich.
eat	

talk about: How many quarters in one flour tortilla. Country where people eat a lot of tortillas and beans. Change in beans from hard to soft after cooking. Smell of garlic, cumin. Other things we mash. What drain means. Other kinds of beans. Other Mexican foods. Another country that touches the United States (Canada). Find Mexico and talk about which country above and below U.S.

vegetable pattycake

The carrots we eat are firm, fleshy roots of carrot plants. Carrots are usually pointy but in some parts of the world, they grow round. And sometimes they are not even orange but white or purple.

(1) **you need:** Carrots, green onion, zucchini (almost any vegetable combination will work), beaten egg, grated cheese (something mild like jack or Swiss), salt, pepper, oil, sprig parsley, wheat germ. Meat grinder with fine attachment, knife for cutting, measuring spoons and cup, grater, oven, bowl, spoon for stirring, muffin tin, liner.

cut	¼ zucchini into large pieces.
cut	¼ large green onion into big pieces.
slice	½ medium carrot into big chunks. (If carrot is bitter, add pinch of sugar.)
cut	1 sprig parsley (fresh).
put	in grinder.
grind	into bowl.
add	¼ cup grated cheese.
sprinkle	salt and pepper.
add	1 tablespoon beaten egg.
add	½ teaspoon oil.
stir	
pour	into lined muffin tin.
top	with wheat germ, about ½ tablespoon.
bake	in 350° oven for about 20 minutes until firm.

talk about: Which ingredients are vegetables, dairy products, spices. What part of wheat kernel wheat germ represents. What happens to cheese. Which is bigger, ¼ teaspoon or ¼ cup. Another way to grind foods (with teeth). Liquid that comes out of the vegetables after grinding.

67

greens
and bacon

**good with cornbread
(made day before)
and/or beans**

Greens are a favorite food in the southern part of the United States. They come from the leafy parts of spinach, collard, mustard, turnip, and chard plants. Some people say the smell of greens cooking is almost better than eating them.

(G) **you need:** 1 bunch mustard greens and 2 bunches turnip greens, all well washed, 5 slices of bacon, salt and pepper, water, sugar. Small, pointed scissors for cutting greens and bacon, electric frying pan, long-handled wooden spoon, measuring cup and spoons, trays to work on.

wash	greens again in running water to remove any trace of grit or sand.
cut	bacon in small pieces with small, pointed scissors. Have children work on trays.
gather	pieces of bacon from trays.
turn	into frying pan and cook until crisp.
remove	pieces from pan (adult job), leaving fat.
cut	greens with same scissors, again working over trays.
gather	pieces from trays into large bowl.
pour	greens into fat.
add	1 cup water.
add	1 teaspoon sugar.
stir	with long-handled wooden spoon, and add water as needed.
simmer	about 20 minutes or until greens are tender. (Greens sold these days are usually tender so 20 minutes of cooking is plenty.)
season	with salt and pepper.

talk about: Different kinds of greens. What happens to greens after cooking. How many pieces of bacon or greens child cut. Which ingredient sweetens greens. What part of plant greens come from. Why they are called "greens."

greens

potato pancakes

① *you need:* Scrubbed potatoes, flour, beaten egg, salt, applesauce, oil for frying. Measuring cup and spoons, spoon for stirring, bowl, wooden spoon, grater, two spatulas, electric skillet, plates and forks.

grate — enough potatoes to make about ⅓ cup. A balance usually works out between children who love to grate and those who would rather not. Have children grate over a bowl so a surplus is ready for those who prefer not to grate.

measure — ⅓ cup grated potatoes into bowl.

add — 3 teaspoons flour.

add — 1 tablespoon beaten egg.

add — ¼ teaspoon salt.

stir

pour — into hot, greased skillet.

pat — out with long handled wooden spoon.

flip — after bottom browns.

remove — to plate.

top — with applesauce.

talk about: Other ways to eat potatoes. Other kinds of pancakes. Other foods we flip and fry. Change in batter from liquid to solid after cooking. Where new potato plants come from (show children the eyes on a potato). Other foods that have vines (sweet potatoes, cucumbers, pumpkins). Other root foods that grow underground (carrots, radishes).

69

eggs

Mother animals lay eggs so babies will grow inside them. Their eggs are full of food that is good for their babies and good for us too. If an animal baby must stay in an egg for a long time before he is ready to hatch, he needs lots of food in his egg. If he's in a short time, he needs hardly any food.

Some eggs stay inside the mother's body while the baby grows. These eggs don't need much food in them either, because the growing babies get food from their mothers until they are born.

Chicken eggs have a hard shell to protect them in case Mother hen sits down too hard while trying to keep her eggs warm. Other eggs, like frogs' eggs, have a sticky covering, so the eggs will attach themselves to rocks where they can hatch more safely.

egg nog

The eggs we buy at the store do not usually have baby chicks inside them because egg farmers hold up their eggs to a strong light and look inside. Fertile eggs, which have the beginnings of a baby chick inside, go back to mother hen or an incubator until they are ready to hatch.

① **you need:** 1 egg per child,* ½ cup milk per child, sugar, vanilla, nutmeg, cinnamon. Measuring cup, measuring spoons, funnel, nutmeg grater (optional), stable bowl that tapers down to narrow bottom, egg beater.

crack	1 egg into bowl.
beat	until bubbly with egg beater.
pour	in ½ cup milk.
add	1 tablespoon and 1 teaspoon sugar.
add	½ teaspoon vanilla.
sprinkle	little cinnamon in.
sprinkle	little nutmeg in (or grate a little whole nutmeg).
beat	with egg beater again.
pour	into cup using funnel.

talk about: What happens to sugar. Where bubbles come from. Smell of cinnamon and nutmeg. Where cinnamon, nutmeg and vanilla come from. Purpose of funnel (to get liquid from large container to small container). Other ways we eat eggs.

*Wash eggs when eating them raw as a safeguard against harmful bacteria.

71

painted cookies

a good two day project

Most of us eat chicken eggs but other kinds of eggs taste good too. Some people eat duck and goose and turkey eggs. Other people love a nice turtle, fish or crocodile egg.

(1) **you need:** Beaten egg, vanilla, flour, milk, melted margarine, sugar, baking soda, salt. Measuring spoons, spoon for stirring, bowl that tapers to narrow bottom, egg beater, cookie sheet, water color brushes, sifter.

measure ½ tablespoon melted margarine into bowl that tapers to narrow bottom.

add 1 teaspoon beaten egg.

add 1½ teaspoons milk.

add ⅛ teaspoon vanilla.

beat with egg beater until bubbly.

measure 2 tablespoons flour into sifter.

add ⅛ teaspoon baking soda.

add 1½ tablespoons white sugar.

pinch salt.

sift onto paper plate, then add to liquid mixture.

stir

spoon onto cookie sheet and pat out to fairly large circle. Leave a lot of space between cookies.

paint with egg yolk paint (see page 73), using water color brushes.

talk about: What parts of egg yolk and white represent (see Egg-in-the-Hole). Other kinds of eggs. Other ways we eat eggs. Other foods with vanilla flavor. How many half tablespoons in a whole tablespoon. Other kinds of paint.

72

egg yolk paint

Children love to watch adult separate yolk from white by passing yolk back and forth between shells. Talk about the different parts of the egg during the process. By five-years-old, some children can do the separation themselves.

To one yolk, add ¼ teaspoon cold water and stir. Divide into 3 parts. Let children add small amount of food coloring to each batch. (Too much coloring makes the paint runny so caution them.) For 20 cookies, use 5 yolks and increase water to 1¼ teaspoons.

egg sandwiches

(1) *you need:* ¼ hard-boiled egg per child, mayonnaise, salt, 1 slice bread per child (children appreciate a choice of breads—whole wheat, rye, white etc.). Fork for mashing or chopper for chopping, spoon for stirring, bowl, plastic knife.

mash or chop	¼ hard-boiled egg. Mashing is slightly easier. After children grow proficient, let them choose their favorite operation.
add	1 teaspoon mayonnaise.
sprinkle	salt.
mix	
cut	1 slice of bread in half.
spread	one half with egg mixture.
cover	with other half.

talk about: Difference between hard-boiled and soft-boiled eggs. How to tell when a liquid is boiling. Other ways we eat eggs. Other things that get mashed (potatoes, fingers in a door). How many halves in a whole piece of bread. How many quarters in a whole egg. What parts of egg represent.

73

egg foo yung

Some animals, like oysters, lay millions of eggs at one time. But chickens think one at a time is enough.

you need: 1 egg per child, shrimp or tuna or both, bean sprouts, chopped green onion, chopped celery, soy sauce, butter for frying pan. Electric frying pan, egg beater or wire whisk, spatula (preferably two), bowl, plates, forks.

crack   egg into bowl.

beat   with wire whisk or egg beater.

add   pinch of tuna, shrimp, chopped celery, bean sprouts, chopped onion.

stir

pour   into frying pan.

flip   with spatula when bottom hardens.

remove   to plate with spatula.

season   with soy sauce and eat.

talk about: Where ingredients come from (tuna from ocean, celery from vegetable garden, onion from root). Which ingredient might make eyes water. Which ingredient child likes best. Names of ingredients (many children cannot recognize familiar vegetables when they are cut up). Seeds at bottom of bean sprouts. Other seeds we eat. What happens to butter. What happens to runny egg mixture. How soy sauce tastes.

quick crepes

If you find an egg bigger than a baseball, it probably belongs to an ostrich who lays the biggest bird eggs around. Hummingbirds lay the smallest eggs—no bigger than peas.

(1) **you need:** ½ egg per child, evaporated milk, flour, salt, brown sugar, little buttter for frying pan. Measuring spoons, electric frying pan or other heat source, 2 spatulas, egg beater.

measure	2 tablespoons beaten egg.
add	2 tablespoons evaporated milk.
add	2 teaspoons flour.
pinch	salt.
beat	
pour	into frying pan.
flip	with spatula to brown other side.
remove	to plate with spatula.
sprinkle	with brown sugar.
roll	up.

talk about: What's bigger, a tablespoon or teaspoon. What makes butter melt. How child can tell when time to flip pancake. What different parts of egg represent. Other things we roll up (sleeping bags, socks, ourselves in covers at night). What happens to runny pancake after cooking. Ways to sweeten food.

75

egg-
in-the-
hole

The white part of an egg is called albumen and it has some food for the baby chicken. The yellow part is the yolk. The small, white strings hold the yolk in the center of the egg where it is safer.

(1) **you need:** 1 egg per child, 1 slice bread per child, butter for frying pan, salt, pepper mill. Biscuit cutter, electric frying pan, two spatulas, cup with pour spout.

cut	hole in bread with biscuit cutter.
fry	bread and "hole" on one side.
crack	egg into cup with pour spout.
pour	egg into hole in bread.
cook	until bottom hardens.
flip	with spatulas.
flip	"hole."
remove	egg-in-the-hole to plate.
cover	egg with cutout "hole."
sprinkle	with salt.
grind	pepper.
eat	

talk about: Egg that escapes around the edges of bread. What makes egg harden on bottom. What different parts of egg represent. How child can know that egg did not have the beginnings of baby chick. Which ingredient makes people sneeze.

dairy foods

Some kids think all milk comes from cows but that's not so. Goat, sheep, camel, reindeer and water buffalo mothers all make milk that people drink in different parts of the world. Milk helps our bones and teeth grow strong.

A cow stores her milk in her udder which has four parts. Each part has one nipple. Pull a nipple; out squirts the milk. Today, dairy farmers have machines with hoses and pipes that suck milk from the udder and carry it to big tanks.

Cows don't eat our way because cows don't have any good biting teeth. A cow must put her gums on some grass and yank her head to pull it into her mouth. She swallows her food after barely chewing it and it travels to the first and second rooms in her stomach which work it over. Then she sends it back up to her mouth where she chews it well. This is called "chewing her cud." Then she swallows it again, and this time it goes all the way through to the third and fourth rooms in her stomach.

What do you think of a cow's table manners?

butter

Butterfat hangs suspended throughout fresh milk and cream in little droplets called globules. When cream or milk is shaken up, globules collect and form clots of butter. Some people call them globs.

(I)
(G)
you need: Half and half or whipping cream,* salt, rolls or crackers. Measuring cup, baby food jars if doing project individually or a large jar with tight fitting lid for a group project, small teaspoon to press out buttermilk.

measure ¼ cup half and half cream or whipping cream.

pour into baby food jar or large jar. Cap tightly. Let it stand outside the refrigerator overnight.

shake until cream clots and butter forms. Work goes faster when done to music with a strong rhythm —and friends' encouragement.

pour off buttermilk and press out any that remains with spoon.

taste sweet butter.

salt to taste.

spread on rolls or crackers.

talk about: How many shakes it took. How many shakes each child did. How buttermilk tastes. Where it comes from. Difference between salted and sweet butter. Difference between buttermilk and regular milk. Change in cream from liquid to solid.

*Make sure cream does not have a preservative added or it will not turn into butter.

my own ice cream

A nicely trained cow comes in from the field, puts her head in her stancheon and waits for someone to milk her. A farmer doesn't have to ask her even once.

ⓘ *you need:* Half-and-half or whipping cream, vanilla, sugar, salt. Small metal juice cans (cardboard does not conduct heat properly), measuring cup, measuring spoons, bowl, spoon for stirring, hammer for smashing ice, plastic bags for holding ice while smashing, container for rock salt-crushed ice mixture (bottom half of half-gallon milk carton is good), wooden tongue depressors (pharmacists carry them).

before: Give each child a couple of adult handsful of ice to smash with hammer in plastic bags closed with wire strip. If child uses small hammer, bag will stay intact.

measure	¼ cup whipping cream or half-and-half into bowl.
add	⅛ teaspoon vanilla.
add	1 teaspoon and ½ teaspoon sugar.
pinch	salt.
stir	until sugar and salt dissolve.
pour	into small, metal juice can.

place

stir

can into larger container and put a 50-50 mixture of rock salt and crushed ice around smaller can. Cover top of can with hand or something else so salt mixture does not get in.

cream mixture with wooden tongue depressor, keeping can surrounded by rock salt and ice mixture until cream mixture hardens, about 10-15 minutes. Add more rock salt as ice melts. Companionship of other ice cream makers keeps interest up over long haul of stirring.

talk about: How mixture changes from liquid to solid. Function of tongue depressor (helps conduct heat out of mixture). What makes ice melt (heat from mixture for one thing, outside temperature for another). Other things that melt (snowballs, chocolate candy held too long in the hand, butter). Other things that harden when chilled (gelatin, popsicles, water). Other foods with vanilla flavor.

81

cheese puffs

(for experienced cooks; takes skill to separate yolks and whites)

The way a cheese tastes depends on how much salt was added, how hot the curing room was, how much whey was drained off, how long it stayed in the curing room, and what the cow ate for lunch.

① **you need:** 1 egg per child, cheddar cheese, sour cream, salt, pepper. 1 tablespoon, 1 teaspoon, bowl that tapers to narrow bottom, small bowl for yolks, egg beater, grater, pepper mill, spoon, cookie sheet.

crack   egg into bowl that tapers to narrow bottom.

lift   out yolk carefully with hand. Or children with more cooking experience may want to separate yolk from white by passing yolk back and forth between two shells until white is all drained off. First method works better if eggs are very cold.

beat   egg white until stiff.

grate   3 tablespoons cheddar cheese.

add   1 teaspoon sour cream.

sprinkle   with salt.

grind   pepper.

mix   gently.

spoon   onto cookie sheet in three mounds.

broil   until tops brown and insides firm, about six minutes.

talk about: What happens to cheese after cooking. Where cheese comes from. Change in egg white. How to tell when egg white stiff. What different parts of egg represent. Another food that gets stiff after beating (whipping cream).

buttermilk puffs

After a dairy farmer makes his butter, he drains off the leftover liquid which is creamy, tangy buttermilk.

(1) *you need:* Flour, sugar, baking soda, salt, nutmeg, oil, buttermilk, beaten egg. Bowl, sifter, paper plate, measuring spoons, spoon for stirring, measuring cup, deep fat fryer, oil for fryer, egg beater, paper towel.

measure	½ teaspoon beaten egg into bowl.
add	1 tablespoon buttermilk.
add	¼ teaspoon oil.
beat	with egg beater.
measure	⅛ cup flour into sifter.
add	1 teaspoon sugar.
add	⅛ teaspoon baking soda.
sprinkle	salt.
sprinkle	nutmeg.
sift	onto paper plate, then add to liquid mixture.
stir	
drop	carefully into hot oil.
cook	about 3 minutes, until golden brown.
lift	out and let drain on paper towel.
cool	a few minutes.
roll	in sugar.

talk about: Where buttermilk comes from. Taste of buttermilk. What makes dough puff (see Watch-the-Bubble-Pancakes). Other foods with tart taste (lemons, vinegar, yogurt). Other dairy foods. Other foods we fry.

fruit flavored flapjacks

(1) ***you need:*** One egg per child, flour, salt, fruit yogurt, margarine or oil for griddle, vanilla, baking powder. Bowl for mixing, measuring spoons, griddle, egg beater, spatula, spoon for stirring, sifter, paper plate.

crack	1 egg into bowl.
add	¼ teaspoon vanilla.
add	1 tablespoon fruit yogurt. (Have several varieties so children can select favorite flavors and try new ones.)
beat	with egg beater.
measure	1 tablespoon flour into sifter sitting on paper plate.
add	⅛ teaspoon baking powder.
pinch	salt.
sift	and add to liquid mixture.
stir	until smooth.
pour	onto hot, greased griddle.
flip	after bubbles appear on surface.
remove	to plate.
top	with additional fruit yogurt. Children who aren't used to the taste of yogurt may want a sprinkling of brown sugar too.

talk about: Other foods that come from cow's milk. Differences between ice cream and yogurt (try to get at tart and sweet and semi-solid vs. solid consistency). Other kinds of pancakes. Other toppings for pancakes. Other things we flip (eggs, cards, stones). How to tell when flapjack should be flipped. How mixture changed from liquid to solid. Sound heard three times in "Fruit Flavored Flapjacks." Another tart dairy product (buttermilk).

84

zucchini pancakes

At cheese factories, workers add rennet, which comes from the lining of a calf's stomach, to milk. The milk curdles which means part of it changes to chunks called curds and part of it turns into thin and watery whey. The whey gets drained off. The curds are cut into strips, salted, pressed into molds and left to ripen until the cheese tastes right.

① *you need:* Zucchini (about ¼ per pancake), beaten egg, flour, salt, little butter for griddle, cheese (cheddar, parmesan, Swiss). 3 tablespoons, bowl, cheese grater, griddle, two spatulas, knives, plates and forks for eating.

grate	1 tablespoon zucchini into bowl. (Zucchini is hard enough to grate but not too hard for small muscles.)
add	2 tablespoons beaten egg.
add	1 tablespoon flour.
pinch	salt.
stir	
pour	onto greased griddle.
flip	to cook other side.
remove	to plate.
sprinkle	with grated cheese of child's choice. Adult will probably have to help younger children grate cheese but they do fine with the zucchini.

talk about: How zucchini grows (on vine along the ground). Other members of the squash family (pumpkin). Another vegetable zucchini resembles (cucumber). What child usually puts on pancakes. Favorite kind of cheese. What happened to butter in frying pan. Other things we flip (pennies, stones).

85

fat pretzels

① you need: Dry yeast, warm water (an electric kettle with temperature control is handy here; otherwise keep adding warm water to maintain temperature), salt, sugar, beaten egg, flour, grated cheese (offer choice of several kinds), kosher salt (coarse grain), beaten egg yolk. Bowl for mixing, spoon, measuring spoons, measuring cups, tray, cookie sheet, spatula, oven, pastry brush.

measure	½ teaspoon dry yeast into bowl.
add	¼ teaspoon sugar.
add	pinch salt.
add	¼ cup warm water.
dissolve	dry ingredients by stirring.
add	1 teaspoon beaten egg.
add	½ cup flour.
grate	about ⅛ cup cheese of child's choice. Try to have a variety and encourage child to taste and select. Hard cheese like cheddar is easier for small children to grate.
add	cheese to dough.
stir	(some children may need help here).
dump	onto flour tray.
flour	hands and knead until dough doesn't stick.
divide	into 2 pieces.
shape	into worms, animals, initials, numbers, whatever appeals.
brush	with beaten egg yolk.
sprinkle	with kosher salt.
bake	in 425° oven for about 10 minutes, until brown.

talk about: Favorite cheese. Why pretzels got bigger (see yeast explanation on Muscle Bread). Other things we knead and shape. Other kinds of cheese. Difference between table salt and kosher salt.

86

pizza for lunch

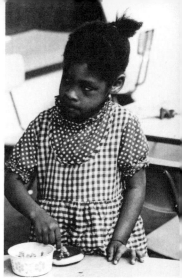

Cows need tails to shoo flies off their backs.

① ***you need:*** Tomato sauce, cheese (cheddar, Swiss, mozzarella), cooked sausage, oregano, chopped green onions, sliced mushrooms, pitted olives, lightly toasted English muffin halves. 1 tablespoon and one teaspoon, cheese grater, portable electric oven (optional but easier).

spread	1 tablespoon tomato sauce on lightly toasted English muffin half.
add	1 teaspoon cooked sausage.
add	4 mushroom pieces.
sprinkle	with chopped green onions.
pinch	oregano.
grate	little cheese and sprinkle on top.
top	with pitted olive. For easy identification of pizzas, write child's name on piece of tape, attach to toothpick, and stick toothpick through olive into pizza before broiling.
broil	until cheese melts, about five minutes.

talk about: What happened to cheese after cooking. Which ingredients are vegetables. Which ingredient loves rainy weather (mushroom). Other things that melt (ice cubes, snow, popsicles). Difference between sausage and hamburger. Other favorite Italian foods.

87

spices and herbs

Many, many years ago, only a few clever men knew where to find spices and herbs, and they sold them for pots of money. These clever men made up scary stories about fire-breathing dragons and five-headed monsters that attacked anyone who tried to bring in spices from the secret faraway lands. Almost everybody was too afraid to look for the land where these precious plants grew but finally a few brave explorers uncovered the secret.

When an explorer brought back a cargo of spice and herb treasures for his king he would say, "Only men with no pockets can unload my ship."

Can you guess why?

He didn't want anybody slipping in a few peppercorns or cloves for his own sausage.

Herbs are mostly the leaves of herb plants but spices come from many different places on spice plants. They can be the flower buds, the seeds, the leaves, the root, the berry, or even the bark of a tree.

mexican cocoa

The Aztec Indians in Mexico were eating chocolate when the Spanish explorers from across the ocean met them. Cocoa pods grow on evergreen trees.

you need: Cocoa or carob powder, sugar, milk, vanilla, cinnamon sticks, marshmallows. Measuring spoons, measuring cup, spoon for stirring, saucepan, hot plate or other heat source.

measure	1 tablespoon cocoa or one tablespoon and 1 teaspoon carob powder into saucepan.
add	1 tablespoon and 1 teaspoon sugar or 1 teaspoon if using carob powder.
measure	⅔ cup milk in measuring cup.
put	1 tablespoon milk from cup into saucepan.
stir	with cocoa-sugar mixture to form smooth paste.
add	remaining milk.
add	¼ teaspoon vanilla.
stir	with cinnamon stick. (Can be used many times.)
heat	until warmed through.
pour	into sturdy cup.
top	with marshmallow.

talk about: Where cinnamon, carob, cocoa come from. Other dishes with cinnamon (pumpkin pie, cookies). Usual way cinnamon comes. What dissolves. Other Mexican foods. Difference between chocolate candy and cocoa.

mulled cider

Cinnamon comes from the bark of the laurel tree. After it dries, it curls up and turns brown.

(1) **you need:** apple juice or cider, honey, cinnamon sticks, lemon. Measuring cup and spoons, saucepan, knife for slicing lemon, spoon for stirring, small strainer, hot plate or other heat source.

measure	1 cup apple cider.
pour	into saucepan.
add	1 teaspoon honey or sugar.
cut	slice of lemon.
add	to cider.
stir	
heat	to boiling.
pour	into cup. Use small strainer to catch peel.
stir	with cinnamon stick until cool enough to drink.

talk about: Other foods with cinnamon. Taste and smell of cinnamon. How cinnamon usually comes (ground). What makes drink sweet, tart. How to tell when cider boiling.

french toast

Spanish explorers named the flavorful vanilla bean pod little scabbard because it looks like it could hold a tiny sword. Explorers tasted vanilla for the first time when they visited Mexico. "Fantastic," they cried and tried to grow it back home in Spain. They didn't know it but the only bee that could pollinate the beautiful vanilla orchid lived in Mexico. And he didn't travel.

(1) **you need:** 1 egg per child, vanilla, nutmeg, cinnamon, two slices bread per child, topping (yogurt, brown sugar, syrup, honey, jam), grease for griddle. Bowl, egg beater or wire plunger (nice change of pace), measuring spoons, spatulas, nutmeg grater (optional), griddle.

crack	egg into bowl.
add	¼ teaspoon vanilla.
grate	little nutmeg or pinch ground nutmeg.
add	⅛ teaspoon cinnamon.
beat	
dip	2 slices bread into egg mixture.
fry	on lightly greased griddle.
flip	with spatulas.
top	with jam, honey, syrup, brown sugar, fruit yogurt.

talk about: Where vanilla, nutmeg, cinnamon come from. Other kinds of toast. Other foods we flip. Changes in color after cooking. Other foods with vanilla flavoring.

hot dog wonton

to celebrate Chinese New Year

① *you need:* Wonton noodles (check specialty shops or regular stores near Chinese community), hot dogs (cut into 5 pieces), beef bouillon cubes, mustard, catsup. Electric frying pan, basket, plates, forks.

place — 1 hot dog piece on center of wonton square.

place — second wonton square over top.

dip — fingers in water.

squeeze — edges of top and bottom wonton together with wet fingers.

put — wonton in basket. To speed process, have children make two.

lower — basket into pan of simmering beef broth.

cook — 2 to 3 minutes.

remove — basket.

turn — wontons onto paper plate.

Have catsup and mustard at eating table and have an adult pour child a cup of peppermint tea from a real teapot to create a special occasion.

talk about: Other Chinese foods. Where China is. What center means. Other things we dip, squeeze. How wontons changed after cooking (hard to soft). Steam from broth. What simmer means (point out bubbles on bottom of pan). Other ways to eat hot dogs.

donuts

**bad for teeth but great for
kindling an interest in cooking**

(1) *you need:* Refrigerated biscuits, sugar, cinnamon, oil for frying. Electric frying pan with basket, paper towel, cylindrical blocks or rolling pin for rolling out dough, pair of tongs or fork for turning donut, bowl.

stretch and flatten   one biscuit from a package of refrigerated biscuits on floured tray. Or use cylindrical blocks to roll out dough.

punch   hole in dough with finger.

shape   into donut shape (any half way reasonable form will do).

fry   in deep hot fat about 2 minutes, turning once (adult job with small children).

drain   on paper towel.

roll   in mixture of cinnamon and sugar. Mixture will stay together better if put in a bowl rather than on a plate.

shake   off excess.

talk about: Shape of donut, frying pan, paper towel etc. Did finger go over, under or through donut? Change in color, texture, size. Smell of cinnamon. Other foods with cinnamon smell. Others kinds of donuts. Other foods that get bigger after cooking (cake, bread, pancakes). How donut feels on hand (warm).

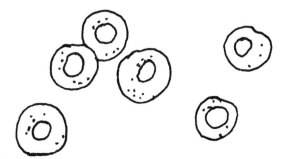

delicious dressing

When two people fight a lot, their friends say, "They are like oil and water." That's because oil and water stay apart from each other. It's very hard to mix them up.

you need: Vinegar, oil, garlic salt, paprika, pepper (in mill), sugar, dry mustard. Baby food jar for mixing, measuring spoons.

measure	1 teaspoon vinegar into baby food jar with cap.
add	½ teaspoon oil.
shake	(so child can see oil and vinegar do mix but not without a lot of shaking).
add	pinch garlic salt.
sprinkle	paprika.
pinch	dry mustard.
pinch	sugar.
grind	pepper.
cap	jar.
shake	
pour	over raw vegetables, salad, or artichokes.

talk about: Which ingredients are herbs and spices. How they grow. Another way that mustard comes. Which ingredients are "hot." Other kinds of dressing.

94

tori yaki

(japanese chicken pancakes)
big enough for lunch

A famous man named Pliny the Elder who lived hundreds of years ago believed herb seeds could cure hiccups. He told his friends, "Drink a few chervil seeds in a glass of vinegar. Chases those hiccups away everytime."

① **you need:** Cooked chicken, beaten egg (½ egg per child), sugar, flour, soy sauce, grease for griddle, sesame seeds. Grinder, spoon for stirring, 2 bowls, griddle, spatulas, measuring spoons, beater.

measure	3 tablespoons beaten egg into bowl.
add	¼ teaspoon sugar.
add	1 tablespoon flour.
add	1 teaspoon soy sauce.
beat	with egg beater.
grind	1 tablespoon cooked chicken into second bowl.
add	to egg mixture.
pour	onto hot griddle.
sprinkle	1 teaspoon sesame seeds over top.
flip	to cook other side.

talk about: How liquid mixture got hard after cooking. Taste of soy sauce. Other seeds we eat besides sesame seeds. Muscles it takes to grind. Another way to grind food (teeth). Other kinds of pancakes. Other Japanese foods. Where Japan is. Other islands. Other products from soy bean (see Apple Soy Muffins).

95

spanish soup for a group

Our table pepper is a ground up berry. Peppers come in all different strengths. Some are so hot, they leave you gasping, "Water, water."

(G) **you need:** 3 large tomatoes, small cucumber, ½ green pepper, ½ red pepper, 3 green onions (tops too), clove garlic, fresh parsley, basil, and dill, olive oil, lemon, two cups chicken broth. Hand chopper, wooden bowl for chopping, kitchen knives, scissors, measuring spoons and cup, squeezer, blender, garlic press, large bowl.

cut	3 large tomatoes into big chunks.
chop	in large wooden bowl with hand chopper. Let children do as much chopping as they want. Blender will finish mixture off.
slice	small cucumber into chunks.
chop	in bowl with tomatoes.
slice	½ green pepper into big chunks and chop in bowl.
slice	½ sweet red pepper into big hunks and chop in bowl.
cut	green onions, tops too, with scissors or knife.
peel	1 clove garlic.
squeeze	with garlic press into vegetables.
put	vegetables into blender and blend until coarse liquid.
add	¼ cup parlsey to blender
add	about 4 leaves fresh basil (or ½ teaspoon dried).
add	1 tablespoon fresh dill (or 1 teaspoon dried).
blend	quickly and pour into large bowl.
cut	and squeeze 2 lemon halves.
measure	½ cup olive oil.
pour	lemon juice into oil.
pour	over vegetables.

add	2 cups chicken broth.
stir	
chill	2 hours or longer.

talk about: Smelliest ingredients. Favorite vegetables. How different vegetables grow. Other soups. Usual temperature for soup. Which ingredients are herbs and spices. Another use for dill (pickles). Other Spanish foods (Spanish name for this soup is gazpacho).

carrot cake

Nutmeg comes inside a fleshy fruit of an evergreen tree. The fruit dries, splits open, and there is the nutmeg. Ginger is the root of the ginger plant.

(I) *you need:* Cinnamon, fresh ginger root, nutmeg (not ground), yellow cake mix, beaten egg, carrots, raisins. Bowl, measuring spoons, grater, muffin tin, liner, nutmeg grater, oven.

grate	about ⅓ of medium sized carrot. Amount can vary pretty widely without harm.
add	3 tablespoons yellow cake mix.
add	¼ teaspoon ground cinnamon.
grate	little nutmeg and add.
grate	tiny amount fresh ginger. A few swipes at grater does it.
add	2 tablespoons beaten egg.
add	6 raisins.
stir	
spoon	into lined muffin tins.
bake	in 350° oven for about 15 minutes, until top firms.

talk about: Smells of different spices. Other recipes that use them. Other ways to eat carrots. Where spices come from. Other foods we grate (cheese, cabbage). Is 5 more than, less than 6.

97

grains

Grains are very important because people eat so much of them. Years ago, people used grain like money. One old time man would say to another, "How much for those boots?"

"One bag of oats," the boot maker would say. "Not a grain less."

Millers grind up some grain seeds like wheat, corn, and rye to make flour for bread. We eat some grain seeds like rice and oats with just their hard outer coats rubbed off.

Grain seeds or kernels as they are also called grow at the top of long stems and have three parts. The first part is called a germ but it's not the kind that causes a cold. This is the part of the seed that grows after planting. As a seed grows, it uses the second part of the kernel for its first food. This second part is called the endosperm.

The third part is a strong covering that protects the tiny seed. Brown whole wheat flour has all three parts of the seed in it. White wheat flour has only the ground-up endosperm. Cows and pigs get the leftover germs and coats because they are full of body-building foodstuff.

rice
pudding

Rice farmers often flood their fields because their plants like wet, swampy places.

you need: Beaten egg, milk, vanilla, nutmeg, brown sugar, cooked rice, cinnamon, raisins. Muffin tin, paper liner, bowl for mixing, measuring spoons, egg beater, pan large enough for muffin tin to sit in, spoon for stirring, nutmeg grater.

measure	3 tablespoons milk into bowl.
add	1 tablespoon beaten egg.
add	¼ teaspoon vanilla.
grate	little nutmeg or add sprinkle of ground nutmeg.
add	2 teaspoons brown sugar.
beat	with egg beater.
add	7 raisins.
add	1 tablespoon cooked rice.
stir	
pour	into muffin tin lined with paper liner. Set muffin pan in larger pan filled with 1″ of water.
sprinkle	top with cinnamon.
bake	in 350° oven about one-half hour, until firm.

talk about: How cooking changed mixture from liquid to solid. What makes pudding sweet. Which ingredient is a seed, a spice. Where cinnamon, vanilla, nutmeg come from. Where rice likes to grow. Other ways to eat rice. Difference between child's age and number of raisins he added.

99

fried rice

In Asia which lies across the Pacific Ocean, people sometimes eat rice for breakfast and lunch and then again for dinner. They eat with chopsticks instead of forks.

(1) ***you need:*** Cooked rice (preferably the day before), bacon grease or peanut oil, chopped green onion, beaten egg, cooked bacon, soy sauce, chopped leftover meat (optional but good). Small frying pan, long handled wooden spoon for stirring, measuring spoons, stirring spoon, bowl, frying pan, hot plate.

measure	½ tablespoon bacon grease or peanut oil and put in frying pan.
add	¼ cup cooked rice.
brown	rice over high heat stirring constantly.
remove	from heat. (Place on protected surface.)
add	1 tablespoon beaten egg.
add	½ teaspoon chopped bacon.
add	½ teaspoon chopped green onion.
add	¼ teaspoon soy sauce.
add	1 tablespoon cooked, chopped chicken, or other leftover meat.
stir	until egg hardens.
eat	

talk about: Color of rice after cooking. What happened to egg. What made it harden. Which ingredients taste salty (bacon, soy sauce). Which ingredient makes eyes water. Other ways of eating rice. Other foods we fry.

brown rice patties

(a large serving for hungry children)

① ***you need:*** Cooked brown rice, chopped parsley, carrots, garlic powder, salt, pepper, flour, beaten egg, soy sauce, grease for griddle. Measuring spoons, spoon for stirring, bowl, grater, electric griddle (preferably sideless), wooden spoon, 2 spatulas, plates, forks.

measure	4 tablespoons cooked brown rice into bowl.
add	1 teaspoon chopped parsley.
add	4 teaspoons grated carrots. (Place grater with bent handles over bowl. Children who don't want to grate can use surplus from those who love grating.)
dash	garlic powder.
sprinkle	salt.
dash	pepper.
add	2 teaspoons flour.
add	1 tablespoon and ½ teaspoon beaten egg.
mix	
pour	onto hot greased griddle.
pat	out with long-handled wooden spoon.
flip	to cook other side.
remove	to plate.
season	with soy sauce.

talk about: Which ingredient is a grain, spice, vegetable. Change in texture, color after cooking. Smelliest ingredient (garlic? soy sauce?). Difference between brown rice and white rice. Other seeds we eat (peanuts, corn). Other foods we flip. Difference between "sprinkle" and "dash." Other foods we grate (cheese, potatoes, cabbage). Why patties are called "patties" (because they are patted out). Other things we pat (animals, heads).

101

applesoy muffins

Soy flour comes from a soybean seed instead of a grain seed. We can eat soybeans the same way we eat other beans too if they are not ground up into flour.

(I) ***you need:*** Beaten egg, applesauce, vanilla, buttermilk, white flour, soy flour, baking soda, sugar, salt. Bowl, spoon for stirring, sifter, paper plate, measuring spoons, muffin tin, liner.

measure	1 tablespoon beaten egg into bowl.
add	1 tablespoon applesauce.
add	½ teaspoon vanilla.
add	1 tablespoon buttermilk.
stir	well.
measure	2 tablespoons white flour into sifter.
add	1 teaspoon soy flour.
add	¼ teaspoon baking soda.
add	2 teaspoons sugar.
pinch	salt.
sift	onto paper plate, then add to liquid mixture.
stir	again.
spoon	into lined muffin tin.
bake	in 350° oven for about 10 minutes, until top is firm.

talk about: Differences between white and soy bean flour. What part of seed white flour comes from. What makes muffin batter grow bigger and lighter (baking soda emits gas that gets trapped inside). What ingredient sweetens. Other things that sweeten. Other kinds of beans. Change in batter after cooking. Other foods that harden after cooking (eggs).

elsie's cornbread

Cows and hogs eat more corn than people. We like corn picked before it's fully ripe so it's juicy inside. Animals prefer their corn hard and dry so they know they've got something between their teeth.

you need: Cornmeal, flour, baking powder, salt, oil, milk, beaten egg, sugar. Muffin tins, liners, spoon for stirring, bowl, egg beater, measuring spoons, sifter, paper plate.

measure	2 teaspoons oil into small bowl.
add	2 tablespoons milk.
add	1 tablespoon beaten egg.
beat	with egg beater.
measure	2 tablespoons cornmeal into sifter.
add	2 tablespoons flour.
add	¼ teaspoon baking powder.
pinch	salt.
add	2 teaspoons sugar.
sift	onto paper plate, then add to liquid mixture.
stir	
spoon	into lined muffin tin.
bake	in 350° oven until top firm, about 10-15 minutes.

talk about: Dry ingredients, wet ingredients. Which ingredient comes from a cow. Other ways we use corn. How mixture changes after cooking. Which ingredient makes muffin puff up (baking powder). Which part of kernel meal comes from. Which ingredient sweetens. Other uses for oils (try to get at machinery: cars, tricycles, sewing machines).

103

one waffle

Farmers plant one kind of wheat before winter. It grows a bit then snow falls like a blanket to protect the tiny wheat sprouts from the cold. Spring comes, the tiny plants awaken and start to grow again.

(1) ***you need:*** Flour, salt, baking powder, sugar, milk, beaten egg, oil. Bowl for mixing, measuring cups and spoons, egg beater, sifter, paper plate, waffle iron (takes a long time, so have several). Turn on waffle iron.

measure	½ cup milk into bowl.
add	1 tablespoon beaten egg.
add	1½ tablespoons oil.
beat	with egg beater.
measure	½ cup flour into sifter (have sifter over paper plate).
add	⅛ teaspoon salt.
add	1 teaspoon baking powder.
add	½ tablespoon sugar.
sift	onto paper plate, then add to liquid mixture.
stir	
pour	into center of greased, hot waffle iron.
bake	until no more steam escapes.
top	with honey, syrup, yogurt, jam, or molasses.

talk about: What makes waffle dough puff up. Where steam comes from (liquid in batter that changes to vapor from the heat). How to tell when waffle done. Number of halves, quarters in one waffle (most irons divide waffles into neat sections). Another kind of iron. Similarity of clothes iron and waffle iron (heat). Change in batter from liquid to solid. What waffle holes are good for (holding syrup).

oatmeal faces

Tiny flowers on the oat plant ripen into oat grains. Horses eat more oats than people do.

you need: Beaten egg, vanilla, brown sugar, baking powder, cinnamon, quick oats, salt, flour, applesauce, raisins. Bowl, spoon for stirring, measuring spoons, cookie sheet, oven.

measure	1 tablespoon beaten egg into bowl.
add	¼ teaspoon vanilla.
add	2 teaspoons brown sugar.
add	⅛ teaspoon baking powder.
sprinkle	cinnamon.
add	2 tablespoons quick oats.
pinch	salt.
add	1 tablespoon flour.
add	½ tablespoon applesauce.
stir	
spoon	onto greased cookie sheet.
decorate	with raisin face.
bake	in 350° oven until done, about 10 minutes.

talk about: Other grains. Other ways of eating oatmeal. Other kinds of sugar. Number of raisins in face.

watch-the-bubble-pancakes

(1) *When baking powder gets wet and hot, it changes into a gas. A gas is like the air you breathe but can't really feel or see. You can watch gas coming from the hot, wet baking powder as the pancake cooks. It starts as a bubble that rises to the top of the pancake. These bubbles hold trapped air inside—just like balloons do—and make the pancake bigger and lighter.*

you need: Flour, baking powder, salt, beaten egg, oil, milk, butter, syrup. Sifter, measuring spoons, bowl for mixing, griddle, knives and forks for eating, egg beater, two spatulas, paper plate.

measure	1 tablespoon beaten egg into bowl.
add	1 teaspoon oil.
add	2 tablespoons milk.
beat	with egg beater.
measure	1 tablespoon plus ½ tablespoon flour into sifter.
add	¼ teaspoon baking powder.
pinch	salt.
sift	onto paper plate, then add to liquid mixture.
stir	
pour	onto greased griddle.
flip	when top is covered with bubbles.
top	with butter and syrup, molasses, honey or jam.

talk about: Where flour comes from. Which part of the seed white flour comes from. Role of baking powder. Other foods that get bigger after cooking (cakes, muffins, bread dough). Foods that shrink after cooking (hamburgers). Another way to trap air inside and make dough expand (yeast, see Muscle Bread). Other things we flip (eggs, pennies).

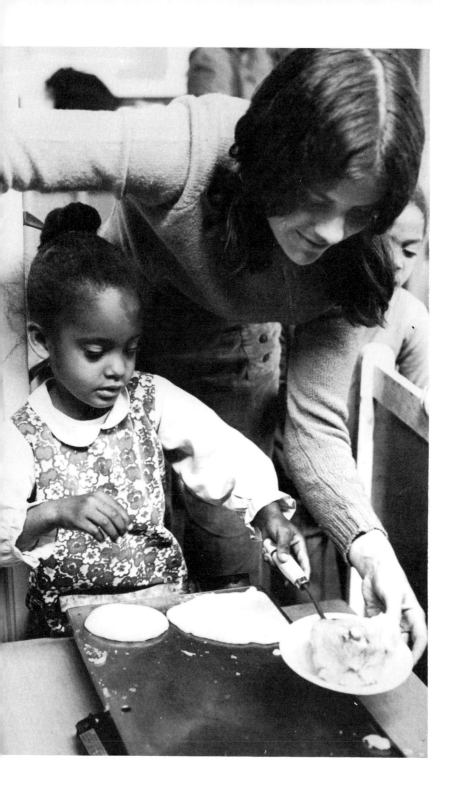

basic cupcake

(1) **you need:** Beaten egg, flour, baking powder, sugar, salt, oil, milk, vanilla. Sifter, bowl, measuring spoons, spoon for stirring, muffin liners, egg beater, muffin tin, oven.

measure   2 tablespoons flour into sifter (have sifter resting on paper plate).

add   1½ tablespoons sugar.

add   ¼ teaspoon baking powder.

pinch   salt.

sift   onto paper plate.

measure   1 teaspoon oil into bowl that tapers to narrow bottom.

add   1 tablespoon milk.

add   ½ teaspoon vanilla.

add   1½ teaspoons beaten egg.

beat   with egg beater.

pour   dry ingredients into liquid (bend plate to make spout).

stir

pour   into lined muffin tin.

bake   in 350° oven for 15 to 20 minutes.

talk about: What's going to happen to batter. What puts air into batter (beating with egg beater and baking powder). Number of dry ingredients, liquid ingredients. What makes cupcake sweet. Other kinds of cake.

biscuit shapes

(1) ***you need:*** Flour, baking powder, salt, oil, milk, butter, jelly or jam (optional). Measuring spoons, spoon for stirring, bowl, sifter, tray, cylindrical blocks for rolling out, simple shape cookie cutters, electric skillet, 2 spatulas, paper plate.

measure	4 tablespoons flour into sifter.
add	½ teaspoon baking powder.
dash	salt.
sift	onto paper plate.
measure	4 teaspoons milk into bowl.
add	2 teaspoons oil.
add	flour mixture.
stir	
knead	on heavily floured tray.
roll out	with rolling pin or cylindrical block.
cut out	simple shapes with cookie cutters. (If the cutters are too intricate, children have a hard time keeping the shape together.)
fry	in well greased skillet.
flip	to cook other side. Shapes can also be deep fried. They puff up and get very crisp on the outside. Both ways are good.
sprinkle	with salt or spread with jelly or jam.

talk about: Which is more, 4 teaspoons or four tablespoons. Other things we knead. Other foods we fry. Other kinds of biscuits. Change in color after cooking. Names of shapes. What makes shapes get bigger.

109

muscle bread

① *Yeast is another way of trapping air inside dough and making it bigger and lighter. Yeast is a very small plant that needs sugar and moisture and a little heat to grow. After it feeds on sugar a while, it makes gas bubbles. The bubbles make the dough grow bigger and bigger until finally the yeast wears itself out. Bakers knead dough to spread the air bubbles evenly throughout the dough. If they didn't, their bread would have big holes in just a few places.*

you need: Dry yeast, dry milk, salt, nutritional yeast or wheat germ, hot water, honey, whole wheat flour, white flour. Medium bowl, measuring cups and spoons, large spoon for stirring, tray for kneading, small pie tins, pan for warm water.

measure	2 teaspoons dry yeast into bowl.
add	¼ cup dry milk.
add	¼ teaspoon salt.
add	1 teaspoon nutritional yeast or wheat germ.
add	⅝ cup hot water.
stir	until yeast and dry ingredients dissolve.
add	2 teaspoons honey (grease spoon for easier measuring) or sugar.
stir	
add	1 cup whole wheat flour.
add	½ cup white flour and mix as much as possible.
turn	onto heavily floured tray.
flour	hands well.
knead	until flour mixed in.
place	dough in greased, small pie tin.
let rise	for 15-30 minutes in pan of warm water. Add hot water every now and again to maintain the temperature.
bake	about 35 minutes in 350° oven.

110

talk about: What made dough expand. Difference between yeasts (nutritional yeast is inactive; active yeast is living and grows, making dough rise). Difference between flours. What makes bread sweet. Change in texture after cooking. Other materials we knead (clay, mud, muscles). What dissolve means.